LAWRENCE *of* ARABIA'S
CLOUDS HILL

Wild mares would not at present take me away from Clouds Hill.
It is an earthly paradise and I am staying here till I feel qualified for it.

T. E. Lawrence to Lady Astor, 8 May 1935

LAWRENCE *of* ARABIA'S
CLOUDS HILL

DR ANDREW NORMAN

HALSGROVE

First published in Great Britain in 2014
Reprinted 2019

Copyright © 2014 Andrew Norman

Front cover illustration by Lynda Appleby

British Library Cataloguing-in-Publication Data
A CIP record for this title is available from the British Library

ISBN 978 0 85704 247 7

HALSGROVE
Halsgrove House,
Ryelands Business Park,
Bagley Road, Wellington, Somerset TA21 9PZ
Tel: 01823 653777   Fax: 01823 216796
email: sales@halsgrove.com

Part of the Halsgrove group of companies
Information on all Halsgrove titles is available at: www.halsgrove.com

Printed and bound in India by Parksons Graphics

CONTENTS

ACKNOWLEDGEMENTS

I AM GRATEFUL TO the following: Bodleian Library, Oxford; *Daily Echo,* Bournemouth; Dorset History Centre; Forestry Commission; Met. Office National Meteorological Archive, Sowton, Exeter; National Cycle Museum; Pen & Sword Books; The Seven Pillars of Wisdom Trust; The Tank Museum, Bovington, Dorset.

Lynda Appleby; Steven J. Barker; Valerie Bedford; Sylvan Bérond; Tom Booth; Peter Bowart; Ed Bristow; Mick H. Burgess; Christopher Donaghy; Nicholas Dragffy; Michael Dragffy; George Forty; Mary B. F. Frampton; Benedicta Froelich; Thomas Gillibrand; Stuart Hannabuss; J. Richard Harvey; Bob Hopkins; Michaela Horsfield; Bill Jesty; Barry L. King; Scotford Lawrence; Den Pechey; Barbara Peirce; Judith Priestman; Robert Pugh; Tosun Saral; Joan Self; Andrew C. Turner; Diana and Alan Turner; Stuart Wheeler; Jeremy Wilson.

I am most grateful to Jonathan M. Weekly, for sharing with me his expertise and for his generosity; to Robert L. Hunt for supplying photographs and granting me permission to quote from *An Handful with Quietness,* and to Louise Seymour-Smith of Wareham Town Museum. I am especially grateful, as always, to my beloved wife Rachel for all her help and encouragement.

ABOUT THE AUTHOR

ANDREW NORMAN was born in Newbury, Berkshire, UK in 1943. Having been educated at Thornhill High School, Gwelo, Southern Rhodesia (now Zimbabwe), Midsomer Norton Grammar School, Somerset, and St Edmund Hall, Oxford, he qualified in medicine at the Radcliffe Infirmary. He has two children, Bridget and Thomas, by his first wife.

From 1972-83, Andrew worked as a general practitioner in Poole, Dorset, before a spinal injury cut short his medical career. He is now an established writer whose published works include biographies of Thomas Hardy, T. E. Lawrence, Sir Winston Churchill, Sir Francis Drake, Adolf Hitler, Agatha Christie, Enid Blyton, Charles Darwin, Sir Arthur Conan Doyle and Robert Mugabe. Andrew was remarried to Rachel in 2005.

Clouds Hill, prior to the rendering and whitewashing of its walls, a tiled roof having replaced the original thatch.

PROLOGUE

Clouds Hill, a cottage, set in the heart of rural Dorsetshire, was the home of T. E. Lawrence from autumn 1923 until his death. He referred to the dwelling variously as follows: 'wonderful'; 'lovely'; 'an earthly paradise'. And yet, it was more than this. For him, it was a place of healing; for despite him being the legendary 'Lawrence of Arabia', he was a much damaged and disillusioned man, as will be seen.

One

CLOUDS HILL, AND
LAWRENCE'S FIRST SIGHT OF IT

CORPORAL LESILE E. GATES of the Royal Tank Corps, Bovington, Dorset (nicknamed 'Tankey'), described how, in the autumn of 1923, Lawrence first came across the cottage, which was to be his future home.

> I remember one afternoon when we were way out over the moors, he [Lawrence] said 'Tankey, what I should like is to find a place, a little house, where I could go and play my records and carry on writing my book.'

This was a reference to *Seven Pillars of Wisdom*, his account of the Arab Revolt[1] (of 1916, against their Turkish occupiers) and the part that he had played in it. Gates continued

> We were walking across the moor up near the village of Moreton and near to the foot of Clouds Hill [a geographic feature which lay immediately to the southwest of the cottage] and we saw a small woodman's cottage. We did after some hard work get the door open. As we went in he said, 'This is my place, Tankey.'[2]

The current inhabitants of the cottage were Staff Sergeant (William) Arthur Knowles, originally from London, his wife Henrietta, and family. He was a veteran of the Boer War and of the First World War (in which he had won the Military Cross).

Henrietta, bore him four sons: Patrick ('Pat', born in 1906), Basil ('Bill'), Richard ('Dick'), and Bryan, and a daughter, Elizabeth.[3] Said Pat

Left: *(William) Arthur Knowles.*

Photo: Robert Hunt

Right: *Henrietta Knowles.*

Photo: Robert Hunt

About two years after the war (the First World War), when Bovington became the depot of the Tank Corps and my father had become the first Pioneer Sergeant of the depot battalion, he started to look around the countryside for a house for us to live in, and with the idea of settling down here eventually when his term of service expired. When he found the cottage, its dilapidated state did not discourage him, and he obtained the option of a lease on it and the small patch of ground surrounding it, from Mr Godwin, the estate agent for the Frampton family, for a few pounds a year, provided that he built an additional bungalow and reconditioned the existing cottage.

The Frampton family, kinsmen of Lawrence, were the owners of the Moreton Estate, upon which the cottage stood.

Before it was finally settled my mother and I came out with him to see the place. We came by way of the camp, and followed a gravel track which narrowed to a footpath and led northwards across the heath, which had become the graveyard of several hundred tanks, being broken up for scrap iron. There were no doors or windows. The roof had fallen in, leaving bare spars against the sky.

(The original roof was said to have been thatched with heather, which grew in abundance on the Dorset heathland.)

Plaster and rubbish littered the floors. A brown lizard cocked an eye at us and scuttled up the wall and two bats hung down from the split oak battens near the chimney stack.[4]

When the school summer holidays came, father took a month's leave. We camped under the hedge and started to clear the site for our bungalow. During the days that followed some of the carpenters and bricklayers who were in the Pioneer Unit came up from camp and helped father with the work. By the end of the month the bungalow, with its corrugated iron roof, was habitable, and mother came with the younger members of the family, to bring us back to an orderly way of living.[5]

The bungalow was situated on the west side of Tank Park Road, opposite to the cottage which was on the east side. The road was so called, because on the east side of the road was an area where, as already mentioned, British Army tanks from the First World War were broken up for scrap.

Pat Knowles then proceeded to give the following description of the cottage and its history. It was set in

> an ever-green hollow, where there is always an overcoat difference in the feel of the weather, in comparison with the surrounding country. Dense thickets of rhododendrons line the hollow and their pleasant greenness relieves the eyes after the monotony of brown and the sun-bleached scars of a man-made desert, where tanks from the nearby camp have churned the heather into submission for a while.
>
> It is sheltered by hills on three sides, and by oak and chestnut trees, planted with purpose, to break the force of westerly gales. In the middle of the hollow, like a sanctification, rises a many-limbed Ilex tree, the Holy Oak of Medieval Lore.[6] Beneath it stands a small brick and clay tiled cottage, with one door only in an otherwise blank wall. It was built in 1808 according to an old diary written by the son of James Frampton, which was found in the local estate office. Frampton gives no reason why the cottage was built, he simply says 'Clouds Hill Cottage built and cottage made', but it is thought that it was to house one of his foresters, who looked after the trees that he and his father had planted; it is estimated that these two Framptons must have planted at least two million trees around the nearby villages of Moreton. Plantations of fir trees remained intact until the First World War, when the trees were converted into pit props and timber to make duck boards (for the trenches).
>
> At the same time the neighbourhood of Bovington Camp became a battle training ground, and the cottage had to be evacuated and was left empty, the first time for a hundred years or more. For about eight years the place remained uninhabited and uncared for. Slowly the home became a ruin, visited by gypsies and tramps, and bored soldiers on an evening out.[7]

Pat then described Lawrence's arrival at the cottage.

> On the day Shaw [Lawrence's assumed name] first came,
> my father and I were painting the outside woodwork of
> the cottage. He asked if it were for sale, or if there was a
> possibility of renting it.

'Shaw' returned the following week and, having considered the matter,
Pat's father Arthur, agreed that he might rent the cottage, together with the
5 acres of land that went with it. Not long afterwards, he moved in. We still
knew nothing about Shaw to connect him with T. E. Lawrence.[8]

Lawrence himself declared that his slender means

> enabled me to take a ruined cottage in a wood near camp, &
> this I'm fitting up with the hope of having a warm solitary
> place to hide in sometimes on winter evenings. This district is
> unusually desolate (of good company) & I covet the idea of
> being sometimes by myself near a fire.[9]

Lawrence named the cottage Clouds Hill, after the name of the hill adjacent
to it, and its vicinity. But how did the hill acquire its romantic name? E. V.
G. Hunt, co-author with Pat Knowles of *A Handful with Quietness*, states as
follows.

> Pat discovered that in medieval times a monk by the name of
> Claude lived the life of a recluse next to the brackish stream
> that passes by Pat's house. The monk was French and the
> correct pronunciation of his name is 'Clowood', hence the hill
> became 'Clowood Hill', which makes very good sense but
> gives something of a let down from the lovely and poetical
> 'Clouds Hill'.[10]

Lawrence explained just how dilapidated Clouds Hill was.

> A tiny brick cottage, with old tiled roof, very high pitched. It
> stands in a thicket of laurel and rhododendron, with oak trees
> and a huge ilex stretching arms over its roof. Damp? Yes; for
> the cottage dates from pre-damp-course days, and the trees
> drip great raindrops on the roof for hours after each storm.

They patter across the tiles like the first notes of the [Beethoven's] Vth Symphony. Only two rooms, the upstairs of the cottage, are habitable. They have three-foot walls, and nine-foot roofs, all open. A great deal of oak and chestnut on show: but my repairs to the roof had to be in deal, which we creosoted to bring it to an ancient colour. My gold Meccan dagger paid the repair-bill, and left something over for furniture.[11]

The dagger, which Lawrence had acquired in Mecca during the Arab campaign, was made to his own specifications.[12]

Said Pat, 'Straightway he got father to knock down a partition in the upstairs room and put a skylight in the roof'.[13] Subsequently, a pediment, carved of stone was set above the entrance door.

At this time, the cottage was of 'brick and tile' construction – in other words, brick walls and a tiled roof. During Lawrence's occupancy, however, the outside walls were rendered and whitewashed.

It was a measure of the warm relationship that existed between Lawrence and his neighbours that the former was permitted to

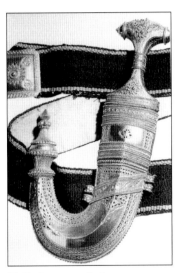

T. E. Lawrence's dagger.
Photo: All Souls College, Oxford

construct a 'water pool' in the Knowles's back garden. This would serve a), as a source of available water in the event of a heath fire and b), as a bathing pool.

For the entrance, Lawrence used two impressive carved doors of teak, which he had brought back from Jidda, Arabia[14] in the summer of 1921. He named the pool 'Shaw's Puddle' after his friend, writer George Bernard Shaw.[15]

Pair of carved doors, brought back by Lawrence from Jidda in 1921. Photo: Ashmolean Museum, Oxford

In June 1924, declared Lawrence

> The cottage is nearly closed in with mountains of rhododen-
> dron bloom, of the screaming blue-pink which I used to
> dislike: now that they are my plants I love them.[16]

In September 1924, Lawrence posed the rhetorical question to Shaw's wife Charlotte

> What is Cloud's Hill? A sort of mixed grill, I fancy, but very
> good. Everybody is beginning to fall in love with it. The air of
> it is peaceful: and the fire burns so well. I'm the only fortunate
> in the camp. The rest burn coal.[17]

Here, it should be pointed out that Lawrence carried very little surplus flesh, and it would therefore be surprising if he did not feel the cold, especially in wintertime.

In June 1925, he told novelist and critic E. M. Forster, whom he had first met in February 1920 at a lunch held in London at a Mayfair hotel for Emir Feisal, that

> Clouds Hill is proud, at this moment, with rhododendrons...
> and the brake [thicket] is full of birds' nests.[18]

Two

LAWRENCE SHEDS HIS FORMER IMAGE AND IDENTITY: THE ARMED SERVICES

O N 30 AUGUST 1922, almost a year prior to having caught his first glimpse of Clouds Hill, Lawrence joined the Royal Air Force (RAF) as '352087 Aircraftman John Hume Ross'. (This was not the first time that he would change his name, as will be seen.) His new life would be quite different to that of his former, high profile existence.

In a letter which he subsequently sent to Dr David Hogarth, he gave his reasons for enlisting.

> The security of it first; seven years existence guaranteed. I haven't any longer the mind to fight for sustenance. As you realise I've finished with the 'Lawrence' episode. I don't like what rumour makes of him – not the sort of man I'd like to be! And the life of politics wearied me out, by worrying me over-much. I've not got a coarse-fibred enough nature for them: and have too many scruples and an uneasy conscience.[1] [i.e. politics]

Archaeologist, senior member of British military intelligence during the First World War, and Keeper of Oxford's Ashmolean Museum, Hogarth was also Lawrence's mentor. In other words, Lawrence was far from satisfied with the role that he had played in the Arab Revolt.

Lawrence's retrospective view of himself as co-leader of the Arab Revolt was in sharp contrast to that which others held of the exploits of the already legendary 'Lawrence of Arabia'. And this legend was enhanced and given worldwide exposure by U.S. writer, broadcaster, and journalist Lowell Thomas. Thomas first met Lawrence in early 1918 in Jerusalem. From 1919 to 1920 he held a series of lectures/film shows in New York and London (and subsequently in Australia, New Zealand, and India), featuring moving pictures and photographs of the Desert Campaign, with musical accompaniment and with himself as narrator. His book *With Lawrence in Arabia*, was published in 1924.

To Lawrence's brother Arnold, the sovereign, King George V, said of Lawrence, 'His name will live in history.'[2] King Feisal subsequently wrote to Lawrence to say

> As a sincere friend of us who has ever been our valuable support, I wish you pleasant long life. [And he ended the letter] I close by reiterating my wishes for your everlasting prosperity and happy days. Your friend Feisal.[3]

Field Marshal Viscount Allenby, Commander-in Chief, Egypt and Palestine, 1917-19, and High Commissioner for Egypt, 1919-25, said of him

> His cooperation was marked by the utmost loyalty, and I never had anything but praise for his work, which, indeed, was invaluable throughout the campaign.[4]

The Emir Feisal, 1919, by an unknown photographer. Photo: Trustees of the Liddell Hart Centre for Military Archives

So why this complete change of attitude on Lawrence's part? Eric Henri Kennington, sculptor and official war artist, first met Lawrence in 1920. In his opinion, the reason was that he

> considered himself fallen from his sublime standard and made the rest of his life an intermittent struggle to reclaim or recreate his soul, by altruistic labour, self-denial and penance. By turns he gained and lost ground, his humble RAF service granted him periods of purification and with them happiness, but never steady strength.[5]

Lawrence's friend Clare Sydney Smith, wife of Group Captain Sydney Smith (Commanding Officer of RAF Cattewater), however, indicated that the adoption by Lawrence of a frugal lifestyle was of a more longstanding nature, related to his admiration for Jesus Christ, the central figure of the Christian faith.

There is no doubt that Tes [her nickname for him], although he could not come to terms with the established religion of the Church, lived a deeply spiritual life based on the life and teachings of Christ. As an undergraduate at Oxford he once sat up all night with a friend discussing on what principle they should base their lives. He himself considered that Christ had lived the most perfect life and he decided to model his on it. Knowledge of this makes his own easier to understand. Having made up his mind to deny the body for the sake of the spirit and to reject the normal man's life of love and marriage, instead of entering a monastery and retiring from the world, he lived a monastic life within the world of ordinary beings. Thus he was able to have a deep friendship for a woman – myself – based on the closest ties of sympathy and under-standing but containing none of the elements normally associated with love.[6]

In March 1923, Lawrence changed course once again, and enlisted in the Royal Tank Corps Training School at Bovington, Dorset as a private soldier, under a new alias 'T. E. Shaw'. He selected this name, he said, not because of his association with George Bernard Shaw and his wife Charlotte, but, as he told the poet and novelist Robert Graves, because it was the first one-syllabled name that appeared on the Army List Index.[7]

Of Lawrence's 'identity change', psychologist and rape-trauma therapist Dr Michael Hunter, in a paper entitled 'The Disputed Sexuality of T. E. Lawrence', stated as follows:

Private 'T. E. Shaw' (Lawrence) with Private Warner at Bovington Camp, photographed by Private Arthur Russell.
Photo: Wareham Town Museum

Psychologists… believe Lawrence changed his name twice because he felt emasculated by his experience [the rape at Deraa] and wanted to escape the macho, action man image being forced upon him by popular culture increasingly obsessed with 'Lawrence of Arabia'.

(This was a reference to the rape of Lawrence by Turkish soldiers under the command of Hajim Bey during the First World War. This, he alleged, took place at Deraain, in south-west Syria, in November 1917, and he gave a graphic description of the event in his book, *Seven Pillars*.)

By changing his name he took on another persona, left the wounded rape victim behind and became someone else for a period of time.[8]

After Lawrence arrived at Bovington Camp, said Corporal Alec Dixon of the Royal Tank Corps, it was some six months 'before any of the rank and file discovered his identity.'[9]

Three
EVERYDAY LIFE AT CLOUDS HILL

ALTHOUGH HIS ADDRESS WAS 'Clouds Hill, Moreton, Dorset', said
Lawrence

> so far as the Post Office is concerned… actually I'm not in
> Moreton parish, but the postman comes on to me from there,
> with his sidecar.[1]

Said Pat Knowles of Lawrence, in the early days

> Sometimes, over weekends, he would sleep there and take
> breakfast in our house because there were, as yet, no facilities
> in the cottage.

Arthur Knowles called his family home 'The Kraal', a name which he
presumably learned during service in South Africa, kraal being Afrikaans
for an enclosure for cattle or other livestock.[2]

> We were often aware of our neighbour in the evenings when
> he played his gramophone, and occasionally we would have
> his company for a meal, after which he would stay and chat
> with my parents.[3]

Lawrence was a devotee of motorcycling and possessed his own machine,
the outcome of which, said Pat, was that all three Knowles brothers,
himself included, 'became motorcycle enthusiasts [as] a direct result of his
influence.'[4]

Lawrence's furniture for the first-floor living room/'music room', which
was set into the eaves of the cottage, included

> a leather-covered settee, for which it was necessary to remove
> a window in order to get it in; a table, two leather-upholstered
> chairs and a plain green carpet. Next came a gramophone and
> books, which completed the furnishing of the one small
> upstairs room to which he came when he had the chance.[5]

Clouds Hill, the Music Room, 1935. Photo: National Trust

In addition, near the door, stood an oak chest, carved by Lawrence himself when he was aged about sixteen.[6]

Lawrence was not only intrigued by wood carving, but also by metalwork, as is indicated by the presence of the following items: a book-rest in stainless steel; a three-piece fender of wrought iron with stainless steel top; a pair of candle holders for the mantelpiece, and a 'beam candle holder' – i.e. to be attached to the ceiling beam, both also in wrought iron.[7] All these objects were designed by him, and the blacksmith at Bovington was commissioned to make them.

Lawrence's gramophone, the very latest machine, was manufactured by E.M.G.,[8] the company having been founded in 1923 by Ellis Michael Ginn of Brighton, Sussex (and subsequently of London). A few years later, Lawrence replaced this with a Columbia Grafonola model, manufactured by the Columbia Graphophone Company of London. He declared that the acoustics of his 'music room' at Clouds Hill were 'wonderful. All my records are there assembled, yards of them.'[9]

Clare Sydney Smith said of Lawrence

He taught me the songs of Delius and Wolf as well as other lieder I had not sung before. He especially liked me to sing Schuman's Cycle of a Woman's Life. He knew Elgar personally and admired his music, especially the Enigma Variations, but he told me that for him, Beethoven held the quintessence of all the composers.

Music and its spell-binding effect on him was something he could never really explain. He tried to once, but could only say it was magic, and like speed it set him free from thinking, but he didn't know how or why.[10]

Apart from Beethoven, the composers that featured most prominently in Lawrence's collection were Bach, Brahms, Handel, Haydn, Mozart, Schubert, Wagner, and Wolf.[11]

The smaller first floor room served as a so-called 'food room'. Here, beneath glass domes, Lawrence kept his bread, butter, and cheese.[12] As for the two ground floor rooms, E. M. Forster stated that in the early days, when he visited Clouds Hill, they were 'full of firewood and lumber. We lived upstairs.'[13]

At Clouds Hill a simple life was the order of the day. Miss Fareedeh el Akle was a schoolmistress who taught at the American Mission School in Jebail. Here, she had first met Lawrence, when he arrived there on Christmas Eve, 1910, during his second visit to Syria. Said she

He was of a very shy, quiet nature and loved to dress very simply, giving little attention to outward appearance. The material things of life had no attraction for him, and money he only valued for its convenience.[14]

U.S. Lieutenant Colonel Ralph H. Isham declared

Once, when we were talking of man's greed, he said, 'The

fools don't realize that their possessions, in time, come to possess them.'[15]

Said E. M. Forster

We drank water only, or tea – no alcohol ever entered Clouds Hill. T. E. always laid in a stock of tinned dainties for his guests. There were no fixed hours for meals and no one sat down.[16]

Fortunately for Lawrence, however, his neighbours the Knowles, kept an eye on him. Said Pat

We always kept his cottage stocked up with consumables – 'C' stores as we called them – such as milk, bread, butter, cheese and fruit, but, regular meals were taken with mother and me.[17]

Pat himself, having worked both on his parents' bungalow and on Clouds Hill, was taught 'the rudiments of bricklaying and carpentry' at Bovington before leaving, in the spring of 1924, for Canada.

As for his fellow soldiers in the Royal Tank Corps, said Lawrence

the cottage is unlike camp, & it gives them a sense of healthy change to visit me, and I like them to like coming.[18]

In an undated letter to Sir Ernest M. Dowson, former Surveyor-General of Egypt, Lawrence declared of Clouds Hill

I'll try to keep it so long as I'm in camp: which will probably be till this time next year, when I'll be due for draft.[19]

But little did Lawrence know just how much his attachment to his new home would grow, as time progressed.

Four

HIS BOOKS: HIS MASTERY
OF FOREIGN LANGUAGES

BOOKS WERE LAWRENCE'S LIFE BLOOD. Once, having proposed to sell his collection, he changed his mind and declared, 'I'd rather keep them than anything I've ever had.'[1]

According to his mother Sarah, as a youth

> 'Ned' could read English easily and his memory was remark-able, any book he took up he seemed to read at a glance, but he knew it all, as I soon found out.[2]

He was an avid reader, particularly of French medieval literature, such as *Chanson de Geste* – 'Song of Heroic Deeds' – featuring in verse, legendary incidents from French history during the eighth, ninth, and tenth centuries.

Three books which Lawrence made a point of taking with him wherever he went, were the *Oxford Book of English Verse*, a *Greek Anthology*, and Thomas Malory's *Morte d'Arthur* – King Arthur being the semi-legendary sixth-century King of the Britons.

Chivalry is defined as

> the medieval knightly system with its religious, moral, and social code: the combination of qualities expected of an ideal knight, namely courage, honour, courtesy, justice.[3]

King Arthur was said to embody all the qualities of the aforesaid ideal Christian knight. However, the Middle East had an even longer tradition of chivalry, which was later embraced into Islam with the advent of that religion in the seventh century.

As a youth, Lawrence declared that he had read 'nearly every manual of chivalry.'[4] Said his mother Sarah when he got older he made long journeys on his cycle to every place in England which had famous brasses of knights; he covered the walls of his bedroom with them [i.e. brass rubbings – the reproduction on paper of monumental brasses], and they made a wonderful show, especially by fire-light: some of them were over life size.[5]

Furthermore, Cyril F. C. Beeson, a contemporary of Lawrence's at Oxford High School, stated Sir John d'Abernon and Sir Roger de Trumpington, both English knights of the thirteenth century, had 'pride of place'.[6]

This being the case, and from what is known of Lawrence's way of life since, it is more than likely that he adopted the chivalric code of the medieval knights as his own.

Arnold Lawrence said of his elder brother, 'He could learn in a few days enough of any Latin or Teutonic language to read its literature'.[7] However, Lawrence subsequently opined that 'there seem to be ten good Greek books to every Latin one.'[8]

Fareedeh el Akle, his teacher at Jebail (1910-1911), stated that

> Lawrence studied Arabic for only three months and notwith-standing the difficulty of the language he made rapid progress; he was able to read, write and speak very simple Arabic in this short time. Lawrence never studied beyond that, although later on when he lived with the Arabs, he could speak their different dialects with ease.[9]

Lionel Curtis, Fellow of All Souls College, Oxford, who met Lawrence in late 1918, soon after the signing of the Armistice, stated that, 'He could learn a language in a fraction of the time that an ordinary mortal would take'.[10] And Clare Sydney Smith declared that Lawrence, 'could speak German as well as French.'[11]

Five

JOHN BRUCE:
LAWRENCE'S ATTEMPTED SUICIDE

JOHN BRUCE, a Scotsman from Aberdeen, in an 85-page account, stated that

> for thirteen years I was Lawrence of Arabia's closest friend
> and associate, during the period of his life from 1922 to 1935.

However, he had delayed publication of his account, having promised Charlotte Shaw and Edward Eliot, Lawrence's solicitor, that he 'would not write about Lawrence while Lawrence's mother was alive.' In the event, Lawrence's mother Sarah, died in 1959, and it was not until May 1968 that Bruce's account was acquired and published by the *Sunday Times*. Its publication would, he said, 'serve to stop the scandalmongers who have delighted in blackening this remarkable man'. Bruce's account, however, showed Clouds Hill to have been the scene of several dramas of an extraordinary and shocking nature.

John Bruce, 1923, provenance of John Bruce.

Bruce had first met Lawrence in London in 1922 at the house of Edward Murray, a friend of his family's doctor in Aberdeen, who worked in the City. When Bruce subsequently came south, to London, seeking employment, Lawrence, he said

> was broke, and unable to earn sufficient to pay his debtors, and there were many. There were vast sums outstanding, and pressure was being applied. That was the reason why he nearly killed himself working all the hours that God sent on the *Seven Pillars of Wisdom*.[1]

Because of his concern for Lawrence, when the latter joined the Royal Tank Corps in March 1923, Bruce volunteered to join with him. However, Bruce was subsequently transferred to 'C' Company, posted to Lydd in Kent, and finally, discharged from the Army, even though he had hoped to remain in the service for another two years. (Bruce, who had expressed to Lawrence the desire to leave the Army, subsequently learned that his discharge had been at the latter's instigation.) However, the two men kept in touch, and Bruce subsequently found work at a garage in Bournemouth [about 20 miles distant from Clouds Hill], where he remained until Lawrence had completed *Seven Pillars*. When Bruce married and announced that his wife was expecting a child, Lawrence volunteered to be godfather.

Bruce's account contained some extraordinary revelations. For example, he stated that Lawrence told him that he had a kinsman whom he referred to as the 'Old Man'. Furthermore, Lawrence had incurred the displeasure of the Old Man, who therefore demanded that he be punished. The punishment was to take the form of floggings, administered by Bruce (much to his distaste). The first of these took place at Clouds Hill in that same year, 1923. Said Bruce

> A birch was used and he got twelve, over his trousers; this did not satisfy the Old Man, and it had to be done again the following week, bare skin this time.

Between 1923 and 1935, said Bruce, a total of nine such floggings occurred. 'The second was again at Clouds Hill in 1924, again twelve, bare skin.' As for Lawrence, he himself recorded in his diary that he had been flogged, not only by Bruce but also by a person whom he referred to as 'G' and whose identity is unknown.[2]

Further light was shed on the floggings by U.S. psychiatrist Professor John Mack, who stated as follows

> Diary jottings of Lawrence, found after his death at Clouds Hill, suggest five incidents of flogging between June and October 1933. Lawrence had noted, for example, 'Saturday 23rd June, 30 from Jock (Bruce's nickname). All of the other floggings were also by 'Jock' (with numbers from thirty to seventy-five indicating, presumably, the number of lashes) except four by 'G'.[3]

I will now turn… to the independent observations of a service companion (i.e. of Lawrence's, who is unidentified) and to material left at Clouds Hill by Lawrence himself.

Lawrence approached this companion in 1931 in great distress, explaining that he had stolen £150 from an 'uncle,' or 'old man,' who came to be known to the companion as 'R'. The Old Man had allegedly threatened to reveal to the world that Lawrence was illegitimate unless he either returned the money, which he was not in a position to do, or submitted to severe floggings. The companion's role was to witness the beatings, and report to 'R' in order to assure that 'R''s instructions were being properly carried out. The presence of the witness seems also to have served the purpose of providing a restraint to any excesses of Bruce's in carrying out the floggings.

The companion observed three beatings with a metal whip between 1931 and 1934. They were brutal, delivered on the bare buttocks, and a precise number of lashes was required. Lawrence submitted to them 'like a schoolboy,' registered obvious fear and agony, but did not scream or cry out. He required that the beatings be severe enough to produce a seminal emission.[4]

Meanwhile, Bruce, in the summer of 1924, (or possibly in the summer of 1925 – no date having been given by him in his account) was invited to Clouds Hill for the week-end, when, he declared, Lawrence

poured out his heart to me, and told me what had been going on, saying it could not go on much longer, as he had again reached the end of his tether.

Having visited the Dorset coastal town of Poole with Lawrence on the motorcycle, and returned to Clouds Hill, Bruce declared

I thought that the ride would have blown away the blues, but no, intuition told me to keep alert. I knew there was a revolver in a chest in the box-room opposite to where we were [presumably a reference to the smaller first floor room], also kept there were the sleeping bags. As the evening wore on, I said I would get the bags ready, I went to get them, and at the same time, I looked to see if the gun was still there. It was, but loaded. This never used to be. I took the bullets out, and took the box with the rest of them, put the gun back, and the cartridges I put into my sleeping bag. There was no lavatory in the house, and before retiring one had to go outside, I went outside first, and when I came back he went.

As soon as he was safely out of the door, I looked in the chest, the gun had gone, I took six cartridges and went down to the door. He had obviously gone further than was the custom, and was away longer than usual. In the still of the night I heard a click. When he did get to the door, I asked if he had been looking for something, he said 'no', I asked 'not even these,' holding out the cartridges in my hand, and in the half light I could see his eyes popping out of his head, then he said, 'Give them to me', and tried to snatch them from me. 'No you give me that right now,' I said, and a little scuffle took place, he trying to get the cartridges, and I trying to get the gun. I bashed his head against the wall until he dropped it, then he cried like a child. I got him up the stairs, but I'm afraid there was no sleep that night. There is no doubt he was ending it [i.e. intending to take his own life] because, the next day, we destroyed eighteen letters [presumably, suicide notes] which he had written to various people, before I had arrived. As I have said, we talked into the early hours of the morning, and he told me how he had been double-crossed [i.e. by the holders of the copyright for *Seven Pillars*, who had stipulated that only 100 copies of the book were to be published. This was a fabrication by Lawrence, who in fact owned the copyright himself].

When Bruce returned the gun and cartridges, Lawrence said 'it's all yours. Take it with you – I don't want to see it again, and you have a solid gold promise, I will never do that again, ever.'

Six

LAWRENCE'S SEXUALITY: HOW CAN HIS MASOCHISTIC TENDENCIES BE EXPLAINED?

LAWRENCE'S SEXUALITY and sexual orientation has been the subject of endless speculation. In December 1927 he told E. M. Forster that 'the impulse strong enough to make me touch another creature has not yet been born in me.'[1] To Robert Graves, in November 1928, he wrote, 'Fucking defeats me wholly. I haven't ever: and don't much want to. So I don't feel I miss much: and it must leave a dirty feeling, too.'[2] 'The period of enjoyment, in sex, seems to me a very doubtful one. For myself, I haven't tried it, and hope not to,' he told writer and critic F. L. Lucas in March 1929.[3] And to Labour M.P. Ernest Thurtle, in April 1929 he wrote

> There is no difference that I can feel between a woman and a man. They look different, granted: but if you work with them there doesn't seem any difference at all. I can't understand all the fuss about sex.[4]

In 1933 he declared, 'I do not love anybody and have not, I think, ever – or hardly ever. Nor have [I] ever, I think, except momentarily-and-with-the-eye lusted.'[5] The sensation of touch, said Lawrence in his book *The Mint*, is the one 'I fear and shun... most, of my senses.' He had never indulged in 'venery [sexual intercourse]... never having been tempted so to peril my mortal soul.'[6] Lawrence 'remained', according to his brother Arnold, 'a virgin until his death'.[7] In other words, even prior to his rape by Turks, the notion of his participating in any type of sexual relationship had been anathema to him.

Lawrence may, therefore, be said to exhibit Sexual Aversion Disorder, the essential feature of which

> is the aversion to, and active avoidance of genital sexual contact with a sexual partner. The disturbance may cause marked distress or interpersonal difficulty. The individual

29

reports anxiety, fear, or disgust when confronted by a sexual opportunity with a partner.[8]

Robert Graves, however, stated that Lawrence had a 'morbid horror of being touched,'[9] and those who knew him well were aware that he was averse even to shaking hands.[10]

The medical term for fear of being touched is chiraptophobia (originating from the Greek, 'chira' meaning – hand; 'apt' – touch, and 'phobia' – fear).

People who have this fear avoid contact with people, which could relate back to sexual fears or fears they could become contaminated. It is believed that heredity, genetics, and brain chemistry combine with life-experiences to play a major role in the development of phobias.[11]

It is therefore likely that Lawrence's aversion to sex was indicative of a wider disorder – namely chiraptophobia.

Is it appropriate to describe Lawrence as a masochist, masochism[12] being defined as 'the enjoyment of an activity that appears to be painful or tedious'?[13] 'Pain of the slightest had been my obsession and secret terror, from a boy,'[14] Lawrence had declared in *Seven Pillars*. Therefore, he cannot be described as a masochist in this sense of the word. However, masochism may alternatively be defined as 'the tendency to derive sexual gratification from one's own pain or humiliation.'[15]

In 1986, Professor Mack met Bruce, now aged sixty-four, in person, and was told by the latter that 'Lawrence seemed to get no pleasure from the beatings'[16] that he administered. However, as already mentioned, Mack stated that Lawrence's service companion had told him that Lawrence had 'required that the beatings be severe enough to produce a seminal emission' – an indication that there *was* a sexual dimension to the proceedings.

At what age did Lawrence's masochistic tendencies first appear? It is known that in respect of the masochist, sexual fantasies are likely to have been present in childhood.[17] Lawrence's brother Arnold, was told by his mother Sarah that Lawrence ('Ned') as a child was beaten 'frequently' by her, such discipline, according to Arnold, taking the form of severe whippings on the buttocks.[18] As for Lawrence, he subsequently described his mother as 'very exciting'.[19] Could it therefore be that the beatings resulted in him becoming sexually aroused?

Lawrence regarded his rape by the Turks as both abhorrent and terrifying. Said he, 'Many men would take the death-sentence without a whimper to escape the life-sentence which fate carries in her other hand.'[20] Nevertheless, when he described how, during the flogging that preceeded the rape, 'a delicious warmth, probably sexual, was swelling through me', this implies an intense degree of sexual arousal, to say the least. It is, therefore, likely that the flogging that he received on that occasion served to reawaken masochistic tendencies which were already present within him. Subsequently, he sought out John Bruce and others to beat him, presumably with the object of recreating that selfsame pleasurable, orgasmic feeling. 'Sexual Masochism is usually chronic, and the person tends to repeat the same masochistic act.'[21]

The means by which flagellation stimulates sexual arousal, orgasm, and seminal emission, doubtless has a physiological basis, in which hormones, notably testosterone, probably play a significant part.

Were feelings of guilt at the heart of Lawrence's masochistic nature – for example, about his having been complicit (unknowingly, at least initially, according to him) in the British betrayal of the Arabs, or for having submitted to his rape by the Turks (even though this was something that he could not, in fact, have avoided, having been taken prisoner)? Probably not, for his masochism appears to have predated these events. However, it suited him to construct a 'script'[22] (blueprint or guideline) for himself, whereby other, self-invented misdemeanours and the resultant requirement for punishment, were woven by him into the narrative of his masochistic fantasies. (A feature of masochists – and also of sadists – is that they typically construct such a 'script' – in Lawrence's case featuring the fictitious persona of the 'Old Man', in order to create a backdrop for their particular brand of sado-masochistic activity.)

Seven

POST-RAPE-TRAUMA SYNDROME: RAPE AS A WEAPON OF WAR

THE PHENOMENON of Post-Rape-Trauma Syndrome is now well documented. In 1980, A. Nicholas Groth and Ann W. Burgess published the results of a study of 22 subjects who had experienced male-on-male rape, of whom 16 were perpetrators and 6 were victims.[1] Victims were compared with controls, and in the former group, the following symptoms were noted:

Anger

> Male victims… seemed to evidence considerable anger at having been raped, and fantasized or planned retaliation against their assailants.

Lawrence demonstrated his anger towards the Turkish bey, when he described him, in June 1919, as an 'ardent paederast'.[2] (Pederasty is defined as a sexual relationship between a man and a boy. But Lawrence produced no evidence to support this assertion, in respect of his tormentor.[3])

A tendency to keep the matter secret

> The male victims felt pressured into not reporting the rape for several reasons: 1) societal beliefs that a man is expected to be able to defend himself against sexual assault; 2) the victim's sexuality may become suspect, and 3) telling is distressing ('It's embarrassing to tell someone you've been raped').

It was not until nineteen months after the rape, that Lawrence first made mention of it.

In an article published in 2005, Jayne Walker, John Archer, and Michelle Davies announced the results of a study of 40 survivors of male-on-male rape, in which the psychological functioning of the victims was compared with that of a control group.[4] The results were as follows:

Self-worth and self-esteem

> The survivor group [i.e. the victims] showed significantly lower self-esteem scores than the controls. There were substantial differences showing that the survivors saw themselves as lacking self-esteem regarding their general competence, their appearance, and in their social lives.

Lawrence repeatedly told Charlotte Shaw that since the rape, he had felt worthless.

Suicide

> Some of the survivors were suffering serious consequences, including suicide ideation and attempts [at suicide].

Viz. Lawrence's attempt to commit suicide at Christmastime 1925.

The long term sequelae of Post-Rape-Trauma syndrome

> Male rape survivors display high levels of psychological disturbance and health problems, even years after the assault.

Their symptoms, which could persist for a decade or more, included social dysfunction, depression, post-traumatic stress disorder, and suicidal ideation and attempts.

It was certainly the case with Lawrence, that his post-traumatic symptoms persisted for many years after the rape.

Feeling dirty

One of the victims stated as follows

> Before the assault I was proud to be a homosexual; however, now I feel 'neutered'. I feel sex is dirty and disgusting and I have a real problem with my sexual orientation.

This is not to imply that Lawrence was homosexual. However, he repeatedly told Charlotte Shaw that since the rape, he had felt unclean.

In late March 1924, E. M. Forster told the poet Siegfried Sassoon

> Have just had four very enjoyable days with T. E. L. I can't understand his attitude towards the body, his own and other people's. He thinks the body dirty, and so disapproves of all voluntary physical contact with the bodies of others. I should like to know whether he held that view before he was tortured at Deraa.[5]

After his rape by the Turks, Lawrence did feel dirty, as he himself admitted in his letter to Forster of December 1927, where he stated that

> The Turks, as you probably know did it to me, by force: and since then I have gone about whimpering to myself, 'Unclean, unclean'.[6]

However, his aversion to physical contact predated the rape.

A loss of direction

Ritchie J. McMullen, author of *Male Rape*, stated as follows

> Being a victim [of rape] means being powerless. It means not being able to control or direct one's body, life, or circumstances. It means lacking autonomy and the freedom to self-govern or self-regulate. It also means not having the power of self-determination….[7]

Lawrence was content to live, thereafter, in relative obscurity in the lower ranks of the armed services; where others would provide his meals, make decisions for him, and in short, absolve him of having to take responsibility for his own life. At the same time, his fellow servicemen would provide him with the companionship which he craved.

Did Lawrence ever come to realize that it was the after-effects of rape which were the cause of his symptoms? Yes, undoubtedly, but perhaps only to a limited extent.

Rape as a Weapon of War

Referring to Lawrence's rape by the Turks, John Godl, in his article 'The

Disputed Sexuality of T. E. Lawrence', stated that

Rape, in time of war... in the military context... was a means of stealing a man's honour, a victorious soldier emasculating a vanquished foe in the belief that by forcibly penetrating him he lost [would lose] his manhood.

The Ottoman Turks were infamous for inflicting it [i.e. rape] throughout the Great [First World] War on captured enemy troops, beating and gang raping enemy officers often as a matter of due course. Prisons and garrisons often had personnel who specialised in this abuse, although there was nothing homosexual about it.[8]

Eight

THOMAS AND FLORENCE HARDY:
NELLIE TITTERINGTON

THE LITERARY FIGURE whom Lawrence revered, perhaps more than any other, was Thomas Hardy. Born in 1840 at Higher Bockhampton near Dorchester in Dorsetshire, the son of a stonemason and amateur musician, Hardy was articled to an architect and spent time as a restorer of churches, before writing the first of fourteen novels *Desperate Remedies*, which was published in 1871.

In 1874, the year he wrote *Far from the Madding Crowd*, Hardy married Emma Louisa Gifford, whom he had met in Cornwall. In 1885, the couple moved into Max Gate, Dorchester: a house which he had built to his own design. There, he wrote *The Return of the Native* (1878), *The Mayor of Casterbridge* (1886), and *The Woodlanders* (1886-7): all of which were set in the West Country – referred to by the author himself as 'Wessex'. A favourite theme of Hardy's was the struggle of human beings against the more powerful forces of nature and the gods.

Owing to the criticism which followed the publication of *Jude the Obscure* in 1895, Hardy decided to write no more novels, apart from his final one *The Well Beloved* in 1897. Thereafter, he devoted himself to writing poetry. In 1910 he was awarded the Order of Merit.

Thomas Hardy and his wife Florence at Max Gate, 15 January 1928, by Emil Otto Hoppe. Photo: Trustees of the Thomas Hardy Memorial Collection

Following the death of Emma in 1913, Hardy, in over 100 hundred poems, expressed the sorrow and remorse he felt. The following year, he married Florence Emily Dugdale, a published author of children's stories who had previously assisted him with research and secretarial work over a number of years.

Lawrence, at his own request, first met Thomas Hardy and his wife Florence, on 29 March 1923 at Max Gate, this being situated only 10 miles from Bovington where he was stationed. Lawrence felt that he could not be a friend of Hardy's because 'the difference in size and age and performance between us was too overwhelming'. And he blamed himself for intruding upon Hardy's presence, and troubling his peace.[1] Nonetheless, he was drawn back to him time and again. Hardy, for his part, did Lawrence the honour of hanging his portrait on the wall of his study. As for Florence, she considered Lawrence to be

> the most marvellous human being I have ever met. It is not his exploits in Arabia that attract me, nor the fact that he is a celebrity. It is his character that is so splendid.[2]

In June 1924, Lawrence invited the Hardys to 'tea at Clouds Hill', which, he told Florence Hardy, would be 'a great honour & dignity for the house'.[3]

Nellie Titterington, parlourmaid at Max Gate, described how Lawrence's visits always livened up the Hardy household.

He had a wonderful sense of humour, at least that is how he looked to me, and I always saw and chatted with him when he came and I opened the door. When he called I always asked as a joke, 'Is it Col. Lawrence, Mr Shaw or Mr Ross today?'; he would smile and say, 'Mr Shaw today'. In front of us maids Mr Hardy always referred to Lawrence as Mr Shaw, and Lawrence always called Mr

Nellie Titterington, portrait by Miss K. H. Maggs. Photo: Mike Nixon

Hardy T. H. when speaking to us or in front of Mr Hardy. Lawrence would come over from Bovington several times a month to talk to him. Indeed, he would never pass through Dorchester without a call and a chat.

Describing Max Gate in normal times, Nellie said

> A gloom filled the whole atmosphere. That's why Lawrence's visits were such a joy to me. He brought happiness for a few moments. Just to open the door to him was a pleasure. He also brought pleasure to Mr Hardy, as did several other of his friends… but apart from these occasions it was a house of noiseless gloom.

What a paradox, that Lawrence was able to bring such pleasure to others, considering the inner turmoil of his own life! Nellie also recalled Hardy's dog 'Wessex', a Caesar terrier, which she described as a 'terror' and 'a fierce, ugly-tempered beast'.

> No guest [at table] could pick up a spoon or anything dropped without the probability of a nasty nip on the hand by Wessex. Hardy could do anything with the dog without any danger, while, if the dog was in a good mood, Mrs Hardy could sometimes pick up a dropped object safely. Col.* Lawrence… was the only one who could safely deal with Wessex: he could pick anything up without any ill humour on its part. Wessex was very fond of Colonel Lawrence, who would pat him and speak to him and had a wonderful sense of power over him.[4]

*Lawrence had been commissioned as second lieutenant in October 1914, and reached the rank of lieutenant colonel in March 1918.

When Wessex died in the spring of 1927, Lawrence wrote at length to Florence Hardy to say what a loss this was to him.

> He was so firm and decisive a being: one who always knew his own mind, and never hestitated to change it, if he thought fit. So doing he showed a very healthy disregard of the feelings of merely temporary visitors. Few dogs appeal to me: but Wessex gained my very definite respect. And the poor old

beast (after I felt so towards him) changed his tone, & became very kind. Max Gate will not seem quite right now.[5]

In the above eulogy Lawrence, with a trace of that sardonic humour for which he was noted, reflected both his affection and admiration for 'Wessex'.

Lawrence was in India at the time of Hardy's death on 11 January 1928,. His heart was buried in the churchyard at Stinsford near Dorchester, and his body was cremated and the ashes interred in Westminster Abbey. 'I wish I hadn't gone overseas,' said Lawrence later. 'I was afraid, that last time, that it was the last.'[6] On his return to England, Florence made him a gift of a coffin-stool and of the great man's fountain pen.

Lawrence with Florence Hardy.

Nine

OU φPOVTIS – 'WHY WORRY?'

IN JULY 1925, into the stone pediment above the entrance door to Clouds Hill, Lawrence carved the following inscription

Ou φpovtis

This is a quotation from the Greek historian Herodotus, which when translated means 'Why worry?'[1] To Lawrence himself, the phrase

> means that nothing in Clouds Hill is to be a care upon its habitant. While I have it there shall be nothing exquisite or unique in it. Nothing to anchor me.[2]

Lawrence's subsequent pronouncements on the subject of Clouds Hill, however, do not bear this out. Instead, they indicate the opposite, i.e. that to him, the cottage was both 'exquisite' and 'unique', and that, as already mentioned, he came to love it more and more.

'Why worry?' suggests that once upon a time, Lawrence did have worries, which he was now attempting to put behind him. But according to Pat Knowles, in this, he was not entirely successful.

> When Shaw was worried or unhappy… it was like feeling a cold draught; he would lean against the mantelpiece of the upstairs room with his hands against his chest, for sometimes an hour, hardly moving except to shift his weight from one foot to the other, talking but little, whilst the gramophone played [3]

So what might these worries have been?

The Arab Revolt

During the First World War, Lawrence, together with Prince Feisal of Arabia, personally led the tribes of Arabia into battle against the occupying Turks. Lawrence himself described how he had spent his time in the desert

riding a thousand miles each month upon camels: with added nervous hours in crazy aeroplanes, or rushing across country in powerful cars.[4]

But the experience took its toll, and Brigadier General Gilbert Clayton, Chief of British intelligence in Egypt, described how exhausted Lawrence was after he had travelled 1,300 miles on a camel in only thirty days.[5] But why did Lawrence choose to ally himself to the Arab cause? Lionel Curtis provided the answer, when he stated that Lawrence, 'once told me that as a child he conceived the dream of freeing the Arab people from the Turkish yoke.'[6]

T. E. Lawrence by Robert Eltham, donated by L. Bayliss.
Photo: Wareham Town Museum

41

Lawrence had visited Syria in the summer of 1909, whilst collecting information for his degree thesis (the subject of which was 'The Influence of the Crusades on European Military Architecture – to the end of the XII Century'). And from 1911 to 1914, when he joined the archaeological excavations at Carchemish, he had learned the ways of the Arabs. When war came, he therefore considered himself to be ideally suited to lead the Arab forces. Furthermore, he knew that his reading would stand him in even greater stead. Said Sir Ernest Barker, his tutor in Modern History at Oxford

> I read the dissertation, which he submitted in the [degree] examination of 1910. It proved conclusively, so far as I could judge, that the old theory of the influence of the castles of Palestine on western military architecture must be abandoned, and that instead of the East affecting the West, it was the West that affected the East.[7]

And Lawrence himself declared

> In military theory I was tolerably read, for curiosity in Oxford years before had taken me past Napoleon to Clausewitz [Prussian soldier Karl Marie von] and his school, Caemmerer and Moltke, Goltz and the recent Frenchmen. These had seemed very partial books, and after a look at Jomini and Willisen, I had found broader principles in the eighteenth century in Saxe, Guibert and their followers. However, Clausewitz was intellectually so much the master of them all that unwillingly I had come to believe in him. Tactically, the only campaigns I had studied step by step were the ancient affairs of Hannibal and Belisarius, Mohammed and the Crusades! My interests were only in pure theory and I looked everywhere for the metaphysical side, the philosophy of war, about which I thought a little for some years. Now I was compelled suddenly to action, to find an immediate equation between my book-reading and our present movements.[8]

> My own personal duty was to command, and I began to unravel command and analyse it, both from the point of view of strategy, the aim in war, the synoptic regard which sees everything by the standard of the whole, and from the point

of view called tactics, the means towards the strategic end, the steps of its staircase. In each I found the same elements, one algebraical, one biological, a third psychological.[9]

In the Arab case the algebraic factor would take first account of the area we wish to conquer…. [Lawrence calculated that] the Turks would need six hundred thousand men to meet the combined ill wills of all the local Arab people. They had one hundred thousand men available.[10]

The second factor was biological…. Nine-tenth's of tactics are certain, and taught in books: but the irrational tenth is like the kingfisher flashing across the pool, and that is the test of generals. Yet to limit the art of humanity seemed to me an undue narrowing down. It must apply to materials as much as to organisms. In the Turkish Army materials were scarce and precious, men much more plentiful than equipment. Consequently our cue should be to destroy not the Army but the materials. The death of a Turkish bridge or rail, machine or gun, or high explosive was more profitable to us than the death of a Turk.[11]

The third factor in command seemed to be the psychological…. It considers the capacity for mood of our men, their complexities and mutability, and the cultivation of what in them profits the intention. We had to arrange their minds in order of battle, just as carefully and formally as other officers arranged their bodies: and not only our own men's minds, though them first: the minds of the enemy, so far as we could reach them: and thirdly, the mind of the nation supporting us behind the firing-line, and the mind of a hostile nation waiting the verdict and the neutrals looking on.[12]

Said Lionel Curtis

Lawrence himself… told me that he spent some of his vacations tramping Syria and thinking out the campaigns of Saladin. When the [First World] War broke out his strategic thinking was already done.[13]

His perceived betrayal of the Arabs

In *Seven Pillars*, Lawrence described looking back to August 1918 and his thirtieth birthday.

> It came to me queerly how, four years ago, I had meant to be a general and knighted, when thirty. Such temporal dignities (if I survived the next four weeks) were now in my grasp – only that the sense of the falsity of the Arab position had cured me of crude ambition: while it left me my craving for a good repute among men.... Here were the Arabs believing me, Allenby and Clayton trusting me, my bodyguard dying for me: and I began to wonder if all established reputations were founded, like mine, on fraud.[14]

At the root of Lawrence's disillusionment was the Sykes-Picot Agreement, of which he claimed to have no prior knowledge.

From 14 July 1915 to 30 January 1916, there was an exchange of letters between British soldier and diplomat Sir Henry McMahon, and Hussein ibn Ali – Sherif Hussein, King of the Hejaz and custodian of the Arab holy cities of Mecca and Medina. The outcome was the McMahon-Hussein Agreement of October 1915, whereby a promise was made that at the end of the First World War, territories formerly occupied by the Turks would be returned to the Arabs. Events would prove, however, that these were nothing more than empty words, for in the meantime and unbeknown to the Arabs, in November 1915, negotiations had commenced between the United Kingdom and France to decide the shape of the Middle East, should the powers of the Triple Entente (United Kingdon, France, and Russia) succeed in defeating the Ottoman Empire. The principal participants were British soldier and diplomat Sir Mark Sykes, and French diplomat François Georges Picot, and the outcome was the Sykes-Picot Agreement, which, made in secret and with the assent of Russia, was concluded on 16 May 1916.

From a perusal of the map which was attached to the Agreement document, it is clear that the division of the post-war Middle East into spheres of influence, was made by the simple expedient of taking a protractor and a ruler and drawing a straight line, commencing in the vicinity of Acre (in the north of present-day Israel), of bearing 060' to Kirkut (in present-day

Iraq). Former Ottoman-controlled territory above this line would fall under French (and beyond this, Russian) influence, whereas territory to the south of this line would fall under British influence.

For the United Kingdom, this would have two enormous advantages. Firstly, a huge buffer zone would be created, preventing any foreign incursion from the east into Egypt and the Suez Canal which was her lifeline to India – 'Jewel in the Crown' of the British Empire. Secondly, the rich oilfields of Mesopotamia would be at her disposal.

The net result was that Lawrence came to loathe and despise the British powers-that-be that had betrayed the Arabs, and felt that he himself had been equally misled and made to look a liar.

The death of Dahoum

It was at Carchemish in 1911 that Lawrence met a youth called Dahoum (meaning 'the dark one'), who made his living ferrying people by donkey to and from the site of the excavations. There was an immediate affinity between the two, and Lawrence made Dahoum his personal servant, a task to be performed by the youth in addition to his other duties.

The 'donkey boy', Lawrence told his mother

Dahoum at Carchemish circa 1912, photographed by T. E. Lawrence.
Photo: British Library

is an interesting character: he can read a few words of Arabic, and altogether has more intelligence than the rank & file. He talks of going into Aleppo to school with the money he had made out of us [i.e. when Dahoum had made sufficient money, it was his intention to attend school in Aleppo]. I will try to keep an eye on him, to see what happens.[15]

Meanwhile, Lawrence asked Miss Fareedeh el Akle, his former teacher, to provide Dahoum with some suitable books with which to commence an education. Also, in the same way that his own father Thomas, had taught him various skills, so Lawrence taught Dahoum photography, and made him his laboratory assistant. However, Lawrence insisted that he remain a Moslem. He would respect Dahoum's faith, and there was to be no question of him being evangelized.

In the summer of 1913, when Lawrence made a return visit to Oxford, he took Dahoum and his site foreman Sheikh Hamoudi, with him – much to the astonishment of the inhabitants of that city. In June 1914, Lawrence returned to England, leaving Dahoum behind at Carchemish. When war broke out in August, the Turks appointed the latter to be guardian of the site, which exempted him from service in the Turkish Army. Lawrence was never to see Dahoum again, for in September 1918, shortly before the Allies entered the city of Damascus, Lawrence learned that Dahoum had died of typhoid fever.

Lawrence's grief at this tragedy is reflected in the following poem that he wrote, dedicated to 'S.A.' – Dahoum's real name was Salim Ahmed – and with which he commenced his magnum opus *Seven Pillars of Wisdom*.

> I loved you, so I drew these tides of men into my hands
>> and wrote my will across the sky in stars
> To earn you Freedom, the seven pillared worthy house,
>> that your eyes might be shining for me
>> When we came

His grief is also reflected in the following copy of a note, which writers Phillip Knightley and Colin Simpson discovered 'among Lawrence's papers in the Bodleian Library…, written by him in pencil on a blank page at the end of Sir Robert Vansittart's *The Singing Caravan*.'

> I wrought for him freedom to lighten his sad eyes: but he had died waiting for me. So I threw my gift away and now not anywhere will I find rest and peace.[16]

A victim of rape

In *Seven Pillars*, Lawrence described how he was captured, flogged, and raped by the Turks. 'In Deraa that night', he wrote, 'the citadel of my integrity had been irrevocably lost.'[17]

Male-on-male rape is not only devastating for the victim at the time, but the experience almost invariably has adverse long-term effects on that victim's psyche, as has already been discussed.

Some have questioned the veracity of Lawrence's account of his rape. However, Arnold Lawrence, hardly a person likely to be easily hood-winked, told Professor Mack (with whom he was personally acquainted), that he himself 'never questioned the factual nature of his brother's account of the Deraa experience.'[18]

Ten

A RETURN TO THE RAF

IN AUGUST 1925, Lawrence succeeded in re-enlisting in the RAF, as 'Ordinary Aircraftman Shaw', and was sent to the Cadet College at Cranwell in Lincolnshire. In his absence, his friend and colleague Private E. 'Posh' Palmer of the Royal Tanks Corps, kept an eye on the cottage for him.

On 26 August 1925 he wrote to Florence Hardy, to explain that his move from Bovington was so sudden that there had been no time for farewells. Nevertheless, he showed that he still thought affectionately of Dorsetshire and of his friends when he said, regretfully, 'Alas for Clouds Hill, and the Heath, and the people I had learned in the two years of Dorset!'[1] In December 1926 he was posted to India.

When Private Palmer left Bovington in early 1927, Lawrence's neighbour Arthur Knowles, took over responsibility for looking after the cottage. It was now to be let, and the income would pay for further improvements, to be made by Knowles. This included the conversion of the larger ground-floor room into a kitchen.

In March 1927, Lawrence's book *Revolt in the Desert* [an abridgment of *Seven Pillars*] was published. That October he was promoted, by reason of his length of service, to Aircraftman Grade 1 (from Grade 2).

In the spring of 1928, Lawrence was concerned that of the two hundred or so Scotch pine trees that had been planted on the hill above the cottage, many had failed to survive. He wrote to Dick Knowles to say

> I want a row of tall, red clean trunks against the skyline, like a cock's comb, on the crest of Clouds Hill, visible from Corfe and from Dorchester.[2]

On 8 January 1929, after only two years in India, Lawrence was sent back to England from his second posting at Miranshah in the north-west. When New York publisher Frank N. Doubleday asked him why he had returned, he said it was

> because the Indians were accusing him of having instigated the revolutions in the neighbourhood and the Russians were

likewise doing so.[3]

In March 1929, there followed one of his happiest postings: to the RAF Flying-Boat Station at Cattewater on Plymouth Sound. The commanding officer was Group Captain Sydney Smith, who had previously been assigned the task of spiriting Lawrence off the liner SS *Rajputana* on his return from India, in order to escape the attentions of the press. Lawrence soon became friends with him, his wife Clare, their daughter Maureen, and the family's retinue of dogs. They nicknamed him 'Tes' (the initials of T. E. Shaw, his adopted name). Lawrence now found himself involved in the development, production, and testing of a new generation of fast and manoeuvrable air-sea rescue boats.

Said Clare Sydney Smith, in regard to Lawrence's physical appearance

> his eyes were his dominating and unforgettable feature. When you looked into his eyes you forgot everything else and he seemed to look right through you. They were a clear light steely blue and set deep under his jutting brow. To my mind none of his portraits give any idea of this strange, compelling look. They may be excellent in detail and general poise but they somehow miss his dominating characteristic.[4]

Referring to the payments Lawrence had received for his translation for a U.S. edition of Homer's *Odyssey* (which he had commenced whilst in India and completed in mid-August 1931, and which was published in the U.S.A. in 1932 by Oxford University Press), Clare declared

> Contrary to popular belief he had very little money when he ceased to be 'Colonel Lawrence'. He had no private means and having refused fat posts and salaries he had to live on his airman's pay. He gave all his profits from *Revolt in the Desert* away, after he had cleared his debt to the Bank. But as he loved books, finely printed ones especially, and classical music for his gramophone, and a fast motor-bicycle, it is quite understandable that he should have wanted to make a little extra money to obtain these luxuries by means of his pen and his scholarship.[5]

In that same month of March 1929, Lawrence arranged for Arthur Knowles to plaster the bedroom walls of Clouds Hill and build 'what he calls a sanitary convenience' on the north side of the cottage.[6]

Eleven

BOOKS: LAWRENCE'S OWN DESIRE TO BECOME A WRITER OR POET

IN NOVEMBER 1932, Lawrence was to say of his books, 'there must be 2000 in the cottage, all going to waste in the hope that I will live there after 1935 when I leave the RAF.'[1]

It is not surprising that works by Bernard Shaw, E. M. Forster, Thomas Hardy, Siegfried Sassoon, Robert Graves, and Graves' mistress Laura Riding (all of whom he knew well and whose company he enjoyed), featured prominently on his shelves. Classical Greek and Roman poets, historians, and philosophers were well represented, as were French writers of more recent times. Such works were usually in translation, but often in their native tongues: Lawrence being familiar with these and other languages.

Other favourite authors were D. H. Lawrence, Ernest Hemingway (whose titles *Men without Women* and *Winner takes Nothing* may have had particualar appeal), James Joyce, Leo Tolstoy, Friedrich Nietzsche, and Robert Louis Stevenson. There were several poetry anthologies, and Moallallas poems translated from the Arabic, as well as Anna Akhmatera's poems translated from the Russian.

There were few books about science and practical matters, except for one about motorboats. His ownership of naturalist William H. Hudson's *Adventures among Birds* (in 24 volumes) and *British Birds* (in 24 volumes), strongly suggest that bird watching was a hobby of his. Also, there were books about war, for example, Winston Churchill's *Marlborough: His Life and Times*, a biography of John Churchill, 1st Duke of Marlborough, and *The World Crisis* (in 5 volumes). Finally, he possessed a copy of the *Holy Bible* and one of the *New Testament*.[2]

In fact, the unsuspecting passer by, who happened to glimpse Clouds Hill through the trees and rhododendron bushes, would never have guessed that within its walls was as fine a library of books as to be found for many a mile.

Said writer John Brophy of Lawrence

> After the War he had tried free-lance journalism. He could
> have obtained high fees for anything to which he would sign
> his name, but rather than trade on his Arabian reputation, and
> in order to find out the true merits of his writing, he sent out
> his manuscripts to editors always under assumed names.
> Every one came back to him with a rejection slip.[3]

In a letter to George Bernard Shaw in December 1922, following his first
meeting with him and his wife Charlotte on 25 March of that year,
Lawrence had said of *Seven Pillars* 'when I finished it I nearly burned the
whole thing for the third time. Is there any style in my writing at all?
Anything recognisably individual?' he enquired.[4] Charlotte was incredu-
lous. 'Now is it *conceivable, imaginable*, that a man who could write the *Seven
Pillars* can have any doubts about it?' she demanded to know of him.[5]

For his part, Thomas Hardy read *Seven Pillars*, and Lawrence was 'very
proud with what he said of it.'[6] As for Winston Churchill, he had the
highest opinion of *Seven Pillars*, of which he would one day write

> As a narrative of war and adventure, as a portrayal of all that
> the Arabs mean to the world, it is unsurpassed. It ranks with
> the greatest books ever written in the English language.[7]

In February 1924 he wrote to E. M. Forster in his familiar self-deprecatory
way, describing himself as an 'imitator' rather than an active writer. He
explained how he had struggled with the book *Seven Pillars of Wisdom*, for
four years 'till I was nearly blind and mad.' He had felt 'profoundly
dejected over it all' and 'the failure of it was mainly what broke my nerve,
and sent me into the RAF.'[8]

Nonetheless, Lawrence continued to seek out the company of writers and
painters. For example, in April 1924 he told Forster, following the latter's
recent visit to Clouds Hill, that he was always

> extremely welcome. Any stranger is, almost: but men who
> write and draw come nearer to my taste than others.[9]

In August 1927, to Charlotte Shaw, Lawrence had declared, 'We misunderstand each other only over my book-writing, which I think is putrid rubbish.'[10] Incidentally, he also described himself as a failed sculptor.[11]

As regards poetry, said Robert Graves

> He was not a poet himself and frankly envied poets. He felt that they had some sort of secret which he might be able to learn for his own profit.[12]

Despite various accolades, Lawrence persisted in believing that *Seven Pillars*, and other works of his such as *The Mint*, were sub-standard. For example to Robert Graves in February 1935, he wrote, referring to *Seven Pillars*, 'Well, I failed in that.' And referring to the time when he and Graves were together at Oxford when the former was a Fellow of All Souls, and the latter an undergraduate at St John's College, he described how he

> was then trying to write; to be perhaps an artist or to be at least cerebral. By measuring myself against such people as yourself and Augustus John, I could feel that I was not made out of the same stuff. Artists excite me and attract me; seduce me. Almost I could be an artist, but there is a core that puts on the brake.

(Lawrence had met the painter Augustus John in January 1919 at the post-war Paris Peace Conference, where the latter was present in the capacity of official artist.)

He could not pinpoint the reason for this. 'If I knew what it was I would tell you, or become one of you. Only I can't. So I changed direction, right, and went into the RAF…'[13]

Twelve

HIS MOTHER SARAH AND BROTHER BOB COME TO STAY

IN THE AUTUMN OF 1930, Lawrence's mother Sarah and eldest brother Bob (a medically qualified missionary with the China Inland Mission), returned to England on holiday and stayed at Clouds Hill.

Meanwhile, Pat Knowles, who had returned from Canada in that same year, observed that

Lawrence's mother Sarah, and his brother Bob. Photo: Jonathan M. Weekly

> Mrs Lawrence and Doctor Bob, no doubt with father's help, had converted the downstairs room into a living-room cum kitchen by fitting a cooking range into the fireplace. The furnishing was kept simple, and with its stone-flagged floor, the effect was not unlike the domestic simplicity of a Dutch interior.
>
> Doctor Bob was studying Chinese for an examination in preparation for an eventual return to China, nevertheless he found time to give lessons in French to [Pat's brother] Bill. On Sundays, he and Mrs Lawrence regularly attended the attractive little church on the knoll at Moreton [i.e. the church of St Nicholas].[1]

During the Lawrences' time at the cottage T. E. Shaw was first stationed at Plymouth and later transferred to Southampton, neither more than a two-hour ride on the Brough even in worst conditions so he was a frequent visitor come to spend a night with his family, or perhaps a flying visit on a Sunday afternoon to have tea with them.

Pat also affirmed that the garage was constructed 'during the period when Mrs Lawrence and Doctor Bob were resident at the cottage.'[2]

As for Lawrence, he declared

> My mother is an enraged housewife. She has cleaned all the cottage remorselessly and takes a pride in polishing it. So there we are! [And he ended] Of course… it is very nice her liking it.[3]

When, in November 1931, Lawrence finally left RAF Mount Batten (formerly Cattewater) for Hythe, Group Captain Sydney Smith made him a present of a hearthrug, blue in colour, with the RAF's monogram in its centre. It would now adorn the fireplace at Clouds Hill, to remind him of the happy days spent in the service.[4] 'Like a cat', he once said, 'I love firesides, and rugs, and quietude.'[5]

In late 1932, prior to the return of Sarah Lawrence and Doctor Bob to China, Lady Astor made them a present of some rugs. As for Lawrence, he made no secret of his regret at their departure.

> I wish these poor things hadn't this cast-iron sense of duty. They are not fit for life in rough places, and they were so quaint and happy in my Dorset cottage, improbable home as it is.[6]

In the event, this was to be the last time that he would see them.

Thirteen
OTHER VISITORS
TO CLOUDS HILL

IN APRIL 1929, Lawrence listed some of the people who had been 'tenants' at Clouds Hill – i.e. who presumably had visited the cottage for a few days or more. They included such colleagues from the armed service as Sir John Salmond (who was appointed Chief of the Air Staff in succession to Trenchard in 1930); Geoffrey Salmond, who succeeded his brother John in 1933, when the latter was forced to retire due to ill health; A. E. 'Jock' Chambers and A. M. Guy of RAF Farnborough. Men of letters included critic and novelist David Garnett; novelist and critic E. M. Forster; poet and novelist Siegfried Sassoon; writer and journalist H. M. Tomlinson; poet, novelist, essayist and critic Robert Graves; Irish dramatist, critic, and winner of the Nobel Prize for Literature (in 1925) George Bernard Shaw. Artists included painters Augustus John and Gilbert Spencer (who spent several months at Clouds Hill in 1924-5), both men being co-illustrators of *Seven Pillars.*[1]

However, his most frequent guests were his friends from the Royal Tank Corps: notably Corporal Alec Dixon, and Privates Arthur Russell and E. 'Posh' Palmer.

In December 1923, when the Shaws were invited to Clouds Hill, Lawrence had expressed a fear to Shaw that his wife Charlotte would 'find it unclean'.[2] The lack of toilet facilities might also have posed a problem! Undeterred, the Shaws duly arrived on Boxing Day. Lawrence was subsequently to confess, 'I don't like women in my place,

Sketch of Lawrence by Augustus John, January 1935.
Photo: Ashmolean Museum, Oxford.

55

anyhow; but I am too perfect the little gent to refuse them.'[3] To him, however, Shaw's wife Charlotte was his confidante, and therefore a very special person.

In late March 1924, E. M. Forster made the first of several visits to Clouds Hill. However, as there was no bed in which to sleep, he chose to reside at the Black Bear Inn at nearby Wool.[4] Said Forster

> we worked for a couple of hours at his book [*Seven Pillars*], then had lunch on our knees – cold chicken and ham, stewed pears and cream, very nice and queer; a fine log fire. I like Lawrence though he is of course odd and alarming.[5]

As for Lawrence, on 6 April 1924, he wrote to Forster to say

> Your coming here was a very great pleasure to myself: and a very great profit, I hope, to that difficult book [*Seven Pillars*] I'm engaged in.[6]

Painter Gilbert Spencer, described the scene at Clouds Hill as he found it in that same year.

> Lawrence squatted Arab fashion on his dais, correcting galley proofs of *The Seven Pillars of Wisdom* which coiled about him snake-like, and finally tailed off among endless dirty black cups and saucers.[7]

War artist William Roberts, who in 1922 created a portrait in oils of Lawrence in RAF uniform, also visited the cottage; he too being a co-illustrator of *Seven Pillars*. Said Lawrence proudly to his friend Private Palmer, 'What a lot of excellencies have eaten toast upstairs there! You and I will eat toast there again, Inshallah.'[8]

Fourteen

FURTHER IMPROVEMENTS
TO THE COTTAGE

I N APRIL 1929, Lawrence told A. E. (Jock) Chambers of the Royal Navy and subsequently of the RAF

> Clouds Hill is still there. I saw it for an hour in February. It is as lovely as ever: only chimney pots are added as a monument to the new tenants' taste.[1]

In September 1919, Lawrence had purchased some land at Pole Hill, Essex – the highest point in Epping forest, where he had built a hut for himself and a bathing pool. Now, in October 1929, he sold the land, with a view to investing the proceeds. This, he hoped, would give him sufficient income for his retirement. 'I am in love with Clouds Hill, my Dorset cottage', he told his bank manager Robin Buxton, 'and have a head-full of plans for it.'[2]

In February 1930, he wrote from RAF Mount Batten to Arthur Knowles.

> It is very good of you to keep the place [Clouds Hill] warmed occasionally. I wish I had the cottage near this camp. For the last four days we have endured an agony of cold.

> There are lots more books likely to follow [a reference to the fact that some of Lawrence's friends had stored his books for him until he had somewhere to put them]. Let me know when the shelving gets full: and then try & find me a chippy [carpenter] to run shelves like the present, but in oak, the full depth and height of the chimney-breast, on each side.[3]

Prior to this, however, it was necessary for the walls of the 'book room' – the larger of the two ground floor rooms – to be cement rendered.

From the autumn of 1930, Lawrence spent time at various other RAF marine establishments, including Hythe near Southampton; Cowes, Isle of Wight; Felixstowe, Suffolk, and Bridlington, Yorkshire.

Clouds Hill, the Book Room, 1935. Photo: National Trust

In November 1930, Lawrence expressed his regret to Arthur Knowles that he had not been able to visit Clouds Hill for the past three weeks. 'How goes the garage? Not going to be an eyesore, I hope?' He then apprised Arthur of

> a moving forest of rhododendron trees coming to you from Derbyshire (rail to Wool, I think) for planting in the neighbourhood of the cottage. Will you find some plant-wise man & and make him put them in at the likeliest places. I understand they are the latest Tibetan and Chinese trees of all sorts of shapes & colours.'[4]

Meanwhile, as already mentioned, Pat Knowles had returned from Canada. This was owing to serious concerns for his father's health. Arthur Knowles died on 1 April 1931, aged forty-nine, his premature death a legacy of his having been gassed during the First World War. Subsequent to this, Joyce Eleanor Dorey, a farmer's daughter from Wood Street Farm at nearby Wool, came to look after his widow Henrietta and her family.

In November 1931, Lawrence declared to Charlotte Shaw, in respect of Clouds Hill

Slowly the certainty that I shall inhabit it permanently sinks in. Once, it seemed incredible that I should have a real habitation.[5]

In November 1932, Lawrence estimated that his cottage contained at least 2000 of his books.[6]

To Florence Hardy in December, Lawrence explained how he intended to use proceeds of his translation of Homer's *Odyssey*, to have the wood beetles, which were eating the roof of Clouds Hill, 'doctored and sprayed', and the kitchen downstairs turned into 'a book-room, with shelves [as previously mentioned].' Finally, if the money lasted, he hoped to have a 'bath and hot-water boiler' installed.[7]

At Clouds Hill, said Pat Knowles

> The only water source, a small brackish-looking stream runs close by the west side of our bungalow, and though brown-stained from mineral trace elements it was wholesome, reliable and constant, and made a superb cup of tea! All water, for whatever need came from there and had to be carried – for thirty yards in the case of the cottage. It was a problem in need of a solution, and Shaw was a man of ideas.[8]

It was therefore necessary to obtain

> a water supply that would cost little or nothing to maintain…. A firm of hydraulic ram-makers was consulted [a 'ram' being a hydraulic machine for raising water] and asked to assess the potential of a spring on the heath nearby. It produced a gallon every seventy seconds which Shaw felt was good enough to work around, but the 'experts' were doubtful.[9]

However, the experts were to be proved wrong!

> Shaw was so certain that it *would* work that he had already gone ahead with his water-heater scheme. The heater, like the ram, is the only one of its kind, *in the world*. It had been designed and built by a Russian engineer [who] had submitted it to the War Office who had turned it down. The results of years of work wasted until Shaw 'came across it' – how I couldn't say.[10]

Meanwhile, local builder William Bugg, was employed to make some further alterations to Clouds Hill. In respect of the 'book room', said Pat

> an oak floor now covered the stone flags; bookshelves lined the walls, and the framework of the large couch which he [Lawrence/Shaw] said was going to make the 'father and mother of all beds', was in place... meanwhile mother [Henrietta Knowles] was making two simple sleeping bags on which Shaw afterwards stitched the words 'Meum' ['what is mine'] and 'Teum' [a mistake by Pat. The correct word is 'Tuum' – 'what is thine'].[11]

In April 1933, Lawrence remarked

> My mother must have put in dozens of daffodils and things, garden flowers, near the house, for the whole of my little patch of grass has been full of them.

However, of this, he disapproved, saying 'Clouds Hill is no place for tame [i.e. not wild] flowers'.[12]

On 31 August 1933, Lawrence described how the new bath had arrived

> beautifully packed, with all its loose parts in another box. It sits in my garage – or garden shed – awaiting the arrival of its boiler-and-burner-and-tank. The erection of the whole unit is to be signalled by an open-to-all bathing festival, lasting one hour. All Clouds Hill will attend, stark naked.

> Meanwhile, we progress. My ram was publicly opened yesterday by the oldest (and only) inhabitant of Clouds Hill, with picturesque ceremony. Less than three hours after the opening ceremony the pipe (100 yards long) had filled and water began to flow into the cottage cistern. A pint came through in just four minutes. The oldest (and only) inhabitant of Clouds Hill took off his RAF cap and drank the pint. It tasted of galvanised iron and red lead.[13]

Also, Lawrence thoughtfully

laid down a spill-pipe, which will feed the kitchen of my neighbour, Mrs Knowles, with my surplus. Both of us are henceforward endowed with running water. We feel so rich and happy.[14]

In late September 1933, Lawrence wrote to his mother to tell here about a new, replacement window in the book room, which

has two fixed side-panes, cemented into the stone frame, and a pivoting centre-pane, in a stainless steel frame. That gives enough light and air to suit me. The other furniture is the window-seat, an affair six feet each way, built up of [his brother] Bob's former bed and a big box-spring mattress: very comfortable and useful.

What used to be the bedroom, upstairs, I am turning into a work-room, to hold a table and papers and ink and food and probably the gramophone and my clothes. That will make the upstairs sitting-room big enough to walk about in.

The staircase has been sheathed in oak three-ply: and the Spenser landscape ['View of Egdon Heath from the Crest of Clouds Hill looking North' by Gilbert Spencer RA] panelled into the gable, quite successfully.[15]

However, on the downside, there were bitter complaints from Lawrence about various books of his that, having been on 'deposit' [presumably deposited with friends], had gone astray. His collection, he said

Was to have been all the worth-whiles of thirty years of reading. There are good things, still, of course – but the incompleteness shames me.[16]

That autumn, he attempted to purchase land on the opposite side of the road from Clouds Hill, in order to prevent further development in that area and to safeguard his source of water. However, the Moreton Estate was only willing to offer him a long lease on this land.[17]

On 11 December 1933, to Lady Astor, Lawrence said, 'I cannot answer your wires [telegrams], because often I have not a shilling to spare.'[18] Was this true?

The answer is yes, because although he had investments worth in excess of £2,000, he relied upon the dividend from this to supplement his pension.[19]

On 21 December, he declared

> I made some money out of a version of Homer's Odyssey in the [United] States, and have put in water, and a boiler and a bath: while the larger ground-floor is now shelved and plank-floored and half-full of books. Upstairs no change, except that I have abolished the bed, and just bug down anywhere, in the rare week-ends I spend in the place.[20]

On that same day, he enumerated Clouds Hill's limitations – some of which were of his own choosing!

> No bed. One sleeps where one can. No kitchen. One feeds in Bovington. No drains. One – under any bush, beyond sight of the windows [i.e. there was no toilet!]. Three of us, a sailor [Jock Chambers], a Tank Corps soldier [unidentified] and myself... assemble here nearly every week-end I can get to the cottage.[21]

On that same day, with his own inimitable sense of humour, and referring to the absence of bed, cooking range, and drains, he declared, 'Give me the luxuries and I will do without the essentials.'[22]

On 26 December, he wrote from Southampton to his brother Arnold. In Lawrence's absence, Arnold and his 'party', which presumably included his wife Barbara, planned to stay at the cottage for a while.

> There is nowhere to cook, in the cottage, and no pots or pans or crockery. No dish cloths – but then, no dishes.

> The upstairs fire burns the best, as yet. I have a stainless steel hood-front coming for the book-room fire which smokes in some winds. There is wood in the woodshed (rhododendron best: the oak is rather green)....

> The cottage has now only two chairs. One for the book-room is being made here, but will not be ready for a week.

I was there over Christmas, with [Jock] Chambers…. The place was lovely; quiet, warm, and full of things to do. I look forward to settling there in a year's time, for good.[23]

On 31 December, Lawrence observed that the cottage

depends for its degree of warmth upon the quantity of firewood its occupant cuts. [However] I cannot light the bath-heater, because of the lack of water.[24]

On 5 March 1934 Lawrence described how Pat Knowles was 'busy roofing in the pool' – Lawrence's bathing pool/water reservoir, situated, as already mentioned, adjacent to and below the grounds of his neighbours, the Knowles family.[25]

In early April, Lawrence apprised his mother of work recently done and of what remained to be done.

Our last doing was to sheath the bathroom walls [the smaller room on the ground floor] in sheet cork [presumably for insulation]. Its grain and colour are beautiful. We have also hung door-leathers [draught excluders, made of hide] to the book-room and the upstairs room, on hinged door-rods of wrought iron. They are in natural cowhide, and very successful.

The upstairs room is complete, but for its beam-candle-sconce [i.e. a candlestick, to be attached to the ceiling beam]. The food room alone remains to arrange, I plan to sheath its walls with aluminium foil; to fit an old ship's bunk across the dark end, complete with drawers: to arrange its food-shelf, its table, perhaps a chair.[26]

This would henceforward be known as the 'bunk room'.

On 26 June, Lawrence wrote from Southampton to E. M. Forster.

I hear that heath fires are raging at Clouds Hill, and am sad and afraid for the little place. I have grown to love it, I fear. What fools we become![27]

In July, Lawrence stated that his income was 35 shillings per week.[28]

On 16 November 1934, Lawrence described how there was no water supply to Clouds Hill, 'while this drought-in-the-deep-springs persists'. As for his sleeping arrangements

> When night falls the cottager takes up his [sleeping] bag, unfolds it on the piece of floor he momently prefers, and sleeps.[29]

Henrietta Knowles died on 20 November 1934 aged fifty-two, whereupon her son Pat, took over the lease on their property.

On 23 November, Lawrence described how, at Clouds Hill, 'for food one goes a mile to Bovington and at sleep-time I take my great sleeping bag, embroidered MEUM, and spread it on what seems the nicest bit of floor. There is a second bag, embroidered TUUM for guests.'[30] On that same day, said he

> I've even saved money and Robin Buxton has invested it for me until it brings in more than 25/- [shillings] a week.[31]

However, on 28 November he declared, 'I had hoped for more, so as to live easily.'[32] As for the cottage, it

> looks simple, outside, and does no hurt to its setting which is twenty miles of broken heath and river valley filled with rhododendrons run wild. I think everything, inside and outside my place, approaches perfection.[33]

In June 1935, Lawrence wrote to his publisher friend K. W. Marshall, in anticipation of the latter's forthcoming visit to Clouds Hill the following month.

> A word of warning. Since [your] last visit the cottage has changed, somewhat. The bed is thrown out. There are two sleeping bags, six loose blankets, and a shabby quilt. Many sheets. A large couch in the book-room, downstairs: enough cushions to pad a man's length of the floor, upstairs – and a narrow long floor-cushion in the food-room (/bedroom,

upstairs). There are no cups or plates yet: but some are on order. I cannot say how long they will take to make them. Six knives, six spoons, six forks. A small kettle: no pots or pans. Enough towels.[34]

E. M. Forster described how, on a visit to Clouds Hill, 'we drank out of pretty cups of black pottery.'[35] The cups had, in fact, been made by Lawrence himself, who described in early March 1934 in a letter to a friend, Miss L. P. Black, how this had come about.

> I have found a pottery near Poole and a month ago I threw a sample cup and saucer, which is drying. When it dries well, I hope to glaze it with galena, a lustrous brown-black which I used with great success before the war for earthenware – and then I shall have a decent tea service.

The creative urge in Lawrence was therefore still very much alive. As for teaspoons to complement the cups, these – four in number, were gifted to him by Miss Black herself.[36] In that year, 1935, Pat Knowles married Joyce Dorey.

Among the pictures which adorned the walls of Clouds Hill were two views of the River Euphrates, painted by Ernest Altounyan's wife Dora, and given to Lawrence by the couple as a present.[37] Lawrence had first met Altounyan, who was now a physician, at Carchemish in 1911. There was also a portrait in pastel of Allenby by Eric Kennington (originally commissioned by Lawrence for *Seven Pillars*, then purchased by Edward Garnett, who gifted it to Lawrence), and a portrait in oils of Feisal, by Augustus John. 'I shall have my dual mastership preserved in my cottage for all time,' Lawrence declared. 'It will be a queer, rich feeling.'[38]

Fifteen

RETIREMENT

IN MID-SUMMER 1933, Pat Knowles commented, in respect of Lawrence's retirement from the RAF, which was due to take place on 26 February 1935.

> Shaw's keen anticipation of living permanently in his home was clearly evident to all, such that, when he said 'only another eighteen months to go,' with such enthusiasm, we all smiled and chuckled, pleased that he was keen to live amongst us as a permanent neighbour.[1]

Meanwhile, the summer of 1934 was the last time that Lawrence would let Clouds Hill to paying tenants. That July, he remarked

> Leisure is the only thing I've never had, and always liked the look of. I think I can use spare time with gladness, ad infinitum: or rather for 24 years, which is my 'expectation'.[2]

He was now aged 46, and his calculation was presumably based on the words from Psalm 90, verse 10: 'The days of our years are threescore years and ten.'

On 3 January 1935, Lawrence declared that nevertheless, leaving the service would be a wrench. 'The RAF's solidity and routine have been anchors holding me to life and the world'.[3] He felt, 'like a snail whose shell is being pulled off him.'[4]

And when the time finally came, he said, as he prepared to bicycle home from Bridlington to Clouds Hill – a distance of about 300 miles

> Out I go. Clouds Hill awaits me, as home and I have nearly £2 a week of an income. So I mean to digest all the leisure I can enjoy: and if I find that doing nothing is not worse than this present futile being busy about what doesn't matter – why then, I shall go on doing nothing. But if doing nothing is not

good – why then, I shall cast loose again and see where I bring up.[5]

On 18 January, Lawrence told his friend Private Arthur Russell

Yes, you must see Clouds Hill this year, if things permit. I have all my books and records there, and love it.[6]

In March, he declared, having now retired

I have saved just enough money to keep me by myself in modest idleness, and I am very much looking forward to doing nothing.[7]

Meanwhile, the press continued to besiege him, and Pat Knowles was often required to act as a decoy, by riding the Brough

around the countryside to draw them off and lose them with a fast run to Blandford or Salisbury. 'The press was responsible for getting me chucked out of the RAF once [said Lawrence], and they might well do it again; and if that happens I have no idea what I shall do.'[8]

On 19 March he informed Pat that he had 'spent all today with Press Association bosses' in an effort 'of persuading all of them to leave me alone'.[9] On that same day, he wrote to Member of Parliament and former Secretary of State Winston Churchill, to enlist his support in putting a stop to the unwelcome attentions of the press.[10]

On 1 April, he said of his retirement

There is pleasure (and engrossment) in arranging and fixing one's surroundings. I find I spend nearly the whole day, beginning job after job and laying them aside, part-done. The sense of infinite time, all my own, is so new.[11]

On 5 April, of his motorcycle, he declared

I've only ridden the ancient-of-days twice this year, It goes like a [military] shell, and seems as good as new.[12]

20 April found him complaining about

> a beastly tit, which flutters up and down one window-pane
> for six hours a day. First I thought he was a bird-pressman,
> trying to get a story.... My time passes between swearing at
> him, cutting brushwood, and inventing odd jobs.[13]

He seemed subdued, when he wrote to Lady Astor from Clouds Hill on 5 May.

> It is quiet here now, and I feel as though I were fixed in my
> cottage for good. It is as I thought... something is finished
> with my leaving the RAF It gets worse instead of healing
> over.[14]

The following day he expressed to Eric Kennington sentiments that, perhaps, many would share after having been retired for a period of two months.

> You wonder what I am doing? Well, so do I, in truth. Days
> seem to dawn, suns to shine, evenings to follow, and then I
> sleep. What I have done, what I am doing, what I am going to
> do, puzzle me and bewilder me. Have you ever been a leaf
> and fallen from your tree in autumn and been really puzzled
> about it? That's the feeling.[15]

On 6 May, he remarked, 'All over bonfires, the beautiful Dorset, to-night. Twenty six, I think, so far, from my window. Ah well, poor George.'[16] This was in celebration of the Silver Jubilee of King George V.

Next day, he told E. M. Forster, in anticipation of the latter's forthcoming visit to Clouds Hill, 'We will try to make you, if not comfortable, at least endurable for a few days.'[17]

On 10 May, he said of Clouds Hill, 'The place is not very comfortable, I fear (and the wish for comfort is not yet strong in me. Frankly I do not aim at it!) and so he [Forster] cannot dare stay long.'[18]

Lawrence was offered the secretaryship of the Bank of England, which he declined. Then Lady Astor invited him to Cliveden (her home in Berkshire) to meet Stanley Baldwin, who the following month would succeed Ramsay MacDonald as Prime Minister. 'I believe when the Government reorganises,' she told Lawrence on 7 May, 'you will be asked to help reorganise the Defence Forces.' However, the suggestion was in vain, for he replied

> No: wild mares would not at present take me away from Clouds Hill. It is an earthly paradise and I am staying here till I feel qualified for it. Also there is something broken in the works, as I told you: my will, I think. In this mood I would not take on any job at all. So do not commit yourself to advocating me, lest I prove a non-starter. Am well, well-fed, full of company, laborious and innocent-customed. News from China [i.e. about his mother and brother] – NIL. The area is now a centre of disturbance. [Signed] TES.[19]

Sixteen
LAWRENCE'S
LOVE OF MOTORCYCLES

DURING HIS LIFETIME, Lawrence was the proud owner of seven successive 'Brough Superior' motorcyles – manufactured by George Brough of Nottingham. His collective name for them was 'Boanerges' – 'Sons of Thunder' – this being the name given by Jesus Christ to his two disciples James and John. Each individual Brough, Lawrence nicknamed 'George' – i.e. 'George I', 'George II' etc.

Sir Ernest M. Dowson, Director-General, Survey of Egypt, described how, in 1913-14, 'Lawrence… used to be continuously at Giza, riding out on his motor cycle Boanerges….'[1] Said Sir Ronald Storrs, Oriental Secretary to the British Agency, Egypt, and Governor of Jerusalem (1917-1926), 'His drug was speed…. He once raced along the open road against an aeroplane and led it for nearly a quarter of an hour.'[2]

Because of his 'addiction to Brough Superiors', Lawrence's fellow soldiers at Bovington nicknamed him 'Broughy'.[3]

Ian Deheer, shipbuilder of Bridlington, said of Lawrence that he had a habit of keeping 'seven or eight half-crowns' in the gauze strainer beneath the petrol filler cap of his Brough motorcycle. 'It saves a lot of trouble getting half undressed to get at your money pocket to pay for petrol etc. on the road,' said Lawrence.[4]

Corporal Alec Dixon reflected some of the joy that Lawrence obtained from motorcycling, when he recalled the summer of 1923.

> We had several outings together on the Brough, two favourite runs being to Salisbury and the Portland Bill. Another favourite spot of his was Corfe Castle, and he usually went there for Sunday morning breakfast if he happened to be free of church parade. Salisbury never failed to delight T. E., and he loved to wander round the Close pointing out the various periods represented in the architecture of its houses. T. E.'s

conversation at such times was anything but dull, for he illuminated those architectural talks with amusing, and often ribald, asides on the habits of medieval priests and nobles. Our visits to Salisbury invariably concluded with a run to Stonehenge, particularly if there had been rain in the late afternoon. He liked to see the place just before sunset when the wet stones took on a purple tinge against the dull sky.[5]

Of RAF Cranwell Cadet College (where Lawrence was stationed from August 1925 until autumn 1926), he declared proudly in his book *The Mint*

The camp wore the virtue of my Brough like a flower in its cap. Tonight Tug and Dusty came to the step of our hut to see me off. 'Running down to Smoke, perhaps?' jeered Dusty: hitting at my regular game of London and back for tea on fine Wednesday afternoons![6]

On 27 September 1926, Lawrence described to George Brough how 'Yesterday I completed 100,000 miles, since 1922, on five successive Brough Superiors…'[7]

In March 1929, when Lawrence arrived at his new station, RAF Cattewater, Plymouth, it was on a new Brough motorcycle – donated to him anonymously by Charlotte Shaw and 'a number of close friends'.[8] Had he purchased it himself, he said, it would have cost 'three years of my pay'.[9] Shaw, however, mindful of Lawrence's many spills, had reservations about it. 'It was,' he said, 'like handing a pistol to a would-be suicide.'[10] The following month, Lawrence described how the Brough had 'taken me twice to London' from Cattewater – a distance of 195 miles as the crow flies – in a 'fastest time of four hours and forty-four minutes.'[11]

Manufacturer George Brough, with Lawrence on his current 'Brough' motorcycle, October 1930.

Photo: Jonathan M. Weekly

In February 1932, Lawrence acquired 'George VII' – a brand new Brough

71

Lawrence and the Brough, 1932.
Photo: Jonathan M. Weekly

Superior, Type SS (Super Sports) 100, numberplate GW 2275 (manufacturer George Brough having taken his previous machine in part exchange).

For this particular model, George Brough, who may be described as an assembler of machines, rather than a manufacturer per se, selected state-of-the-art components from several different manufacturers, for example:

Engine – JAP 998 cc air-cooled, twin cam, overhead valve, by J. A. Prestwick of Tottenham, London
Carburettor – by AMAL
Gearbox – 3-speed, manual, by Sturmey Archer
Frame – cantilever-sprung suspension by Bentley and Draper
Brakes and wheels – by Enfield
Dynamo, headlamps and horn – by Lucas
Front forks – by Castle Brampton, from a design by Harley Davidson
Oil pump – by Pilgrim
Chain – by Coventry
Saddle – by Lycett Aero

In addition, the following, non-standard features were included at Lawrence's own request:

Rear wheel – 19-inch diameter, instead of a 21-inch, to suit his relatively small frame.
Petrol tank in stainless steel – by Skegness Sheet Metal Works
Speedometer – 120 mph by Jaeger
Muffler – fitted to the carburettor to prevent icing up[12]

The Brough was also equipped with an inflatable cushion, fitted to the pillion passenger seat for greater comfort; large alpine carrier and bags with valises; a small toolbox, fitted low down on the nearside. In a letter sent to George Brough after taking delivery, he described it as 'the silkiest thing I have ever ridden.'[13]

The Brough Type SS100, however, for all its legendary status, had a serious flaw, in that the front brakes, manufactured by Royal Enfield, were incompatible with the front forks, manufactured by Castle Brampton, as far as the fitting of one to the other was concerned. The outcome was that, unlike the rear brakes which were thoroughly efficient, this was not the case with the front ones.

The tax disc for Lawrence's final Brough. Photo: Jonathan M. Weekly

On 3 May 1934, Lawrence wrote to George Brough, prophetically as it transpired, to say

> My last two long rides have been at 49 and 51 mph respectively. It looks as though I might yet break my neck on a B. S. ['Brough Superior'].[14]

To Charlotte Shaw on 31 December, eight weeks before he was due to retire from the RAF, Lawrence wrote to describe the journey north from Clouds Hill.

> The Brough purred smoothly, to Royston and Biggleswade and Stamford and Grantham and Bawtry and Goole and Bridlington. Even the rain ceased after a while, and I got in warm and dry. Today I have cleaned the good servant till it shines again. All the last two months it has been stored at Clouds Hill, until I felt that it had almost shared my unhappiness in our separation.[15]

Devoted as Lawrence was to his Broughs, there was a downside to his motorcyling activities; for although manufacturer George Brough stated that he never saw Lawrence 'take a single risk nor put any other rider or driver to the slightest inconvenience,'[16] the evidence does not bear this out. For example, on 10 December 1925 Lawrence stated that he had

> crashed off the Brough last Monday: knee: ankle; elbow: being repaired [presumably a reference to the Brough!]. Tunic and breeches being replaced. Front mudguard, name-plate, handlebars, footrest, renewed. Skid on ice at 55 m.p.h. Dark: wet: most miserable. Hobble like a cripple now.[17]

Said Pat Knowles

> During those last years, he was involved in several more-or-less serious accidents. It got so that each time he came I used to scan the bike for damage… One afternoon we heard him arrive – the Brough's engine is unmistakable – but instead of going to the garage [at the rear of Clouds Hill] as he usually did he stopped outside our house and hooted, so I went out to see what was wrong.
>
> He was clearly in pain and he was sitting uncomfortably. I also noticed a buckled footrest. I helped him to put the bike away and he was able to walk unsupported to the cottage, where with difficulty we got his top clothes off to inspect the damage. He was extensively bruised.[18]

Meanwhile, an eighth Brough was on order from the manufacturers.[19]

Seventeen

THE CRASH

O N MONDAY 13 May 1935, Lawrence motorcycled from Clouds Hill southwards, along down Tank Park Road to Bovington Post Office, to send off a parcel of books and a telegram. The intended recipient was the author Henry Williamson, about whose book *Tarka the Otter*, he had written a long and detailed critique which Williamson had much appreciated.

The telegram was in response to a letter from Williamson in which the latter had declared

> The new age must begin: Europe was ready for peace: Lawrence was the natural leader of that age in England. I dreamed of an Anglo-German friendship, the beginning of the pacification of Europe. Hitler and Lawrence must meet. I wrote thus to him, shortly after he had left the RAF.[1]

Bovington in the 1930s, the Red Garage right foreground. Photo: Jonathan M. Weekly

Lawrence's telegram read, 'Lunch Tuesday wet fine cottage 1 mile North Bovington Camp.'

Bovington Post Office.
Photo: Jonathan M. Weekly

However, the two men were destined not to meet, for on his return journey, he collided with boy cyclist Albert Hargraves or 'Bert', a butcher's errand boy whose father, also Albert, was a soldier at Bovington Camp. Bert was accompanied by his friend Frank Fletcher, who had gone along with him to keep him company. The outcome was that Lawrence sustained injuries, from which he died six days later (on Sunday 19 May), without regaining consciousness. As the post-mortem confirmed, the cause of death was brain damage due to a fractured skull. There was no mention of any other injuries. At the inquest, held on 21 May, the coroner's jury brought in a verdict of accidental death.[2]

As for errand boy Hargraves, although 'not seriously injured', he was, nevertheless, detained in hospital for several days.[3]

'On the evening before the accident,' said Pat Knowles, poignantly

> after we had had our evening meal we went and sat on the hilltop and talked, our conversation ranged from Maiden

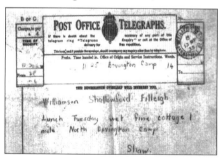

Above: *Telegram, sent by Lawrence to Henry Williamson on morning of crash.*
Photo: Jonathan M. Weekly
Right: *Albert ('Bert') Hargraves, aged fourteen, on day of inquest.*

Lawrence's Brough motorcycle being unloaded at Bovington Camp on morning of inquest by Private Arthur Russell. Photo: Jonathan M. Weekly

Castle to Bridport and from Culliford Clump to Hardy's 'Dynasts', which was one of Shaw's favourite epic poems.

It seemed that our plans to start up our small printing press would have to be put on hold for a year or two because he was expecting to be asked to undertake work of national importance, work relating to Home Defence. [With the printing press, Lawrence planned to produce 'a few copies (perhaps as many as a hundred)' of *The Mint*.][4] He seemed really contented and happy and I later went to my house with the feeling that he had at last settled down to an easy stretch of living.

The next morning he came across to my house earlier than usual. Whilst I was getting breakfast the postman came. Shaw opened his mail and said that Williamson wanted to see him. Over breakfast we discussed his [Williamson's] letter. Shaw felt that it would be as well to let him come as soon as possible as he might not have the time to spare later. I said why not the next day? He thought it a good idea, and so it was decided; he would go down later and send off a telegram telling him to come for lunch the following day.[5]

After breakfast Shaw brought out the Brough and I heard him running it up [preparing the engine]. I guessed he was cleaning and polishing and servicing it. About mid-morning he came across to asked if there was anything he could get for me whilst he was in Bovington. I was working in the garden and heard him leave and heard the sound of the Brough's engine all the way to Bovington. The wind was light and from the south, and, believe it or not, but I could even hear the sounds of the parade-sergeants on the square… Much later I became aware of the Brough's engine again. I heard it rev-up as though he was changing gear, and thought 'Hullo, he's stopped to chat to someone,' – something he liked to do, and thought no more about it.

The next thing to disturb my peace was an R.A.M.C. [Royal Army Medical Corps] sergeant who came running down my garden path. He said that there had been an accident and asked me to come and identify the injured man.[6]

On seeing his friend in such a parlous state, Pat's thoughts can only be imagined.

Corporal Ernest Catchpole of The Royal Army Ordnance Corps, stationed at Tidworth, Wiltshire, stated at the inquest into Lawrence's death that

At about 11.20 a.m. on May 13th 1935, I was at Clouds Hill Camping Ground [a tented military summer camp, otherwise known as 'Wool Camp'] and about 100 yards from the road. I heard the noise of a motorcycle coming from the direction of Bovington Camp. I saw the motorcycle which was going between 50 and 60 miles an hour. Just before the motorcycle got level with the camp it passed a black car – it was a private car and the motorcycle passed that safely. I then saw the motorcyclist swerve across the road to avoid two pedal cyclists going in the same direction. The motorcyclist swerved immediately after he passed the car which was going in the opposite direction. I then heard a crash and saw the motorcy-cle twisting and turning over and over along the road.

I immediately went to the road and called for help. I found the motorcyclist lying on the right side of the road – his face was covered in blood

The car was not going very fast. I actually saw the deceased pass the car. I should say the collision occurred about 15 to 20 feet after the motorcyclist had passed the car. I do not know whether the pedal cyclists were riding one behind the other or abreast. There would have been sufficient room for the motor-cyclist to pass between the car and the pedal cyclists if the motorcyclist had not been going at such a speed. I did not see the pedal-cyclists before the crash. The car was on its proper [i.e. left hand] side of the road.

In other words, according to Catchpole,[7] when the collision occurred the distance between the car and the rearmost bicycle was not more than two or three times the length of the Brough (i.e. 15-21 feet, the Brough being 7½ feet long).

Said fourteen-year-old Frank Fletcher

On 13th May 1935 at about 11.20 a.m., I was riding a pedal bicycle from Bovington Camp towards Clouds Hill and Albert Hargraves was with me. I was riding in front and Hargraves was riding at the back. I was riding on the left of the road. When opposite Clouds Hill Camp I heard a motorcycle coming from behind. I then heard a crash and Bert's bicycle fell on top of me and knocked me off my bicycle. I got up and saw Mr Lawrence go over the handlebars of the motorcycle and fall about five yards in front.

Frank Fletcher.

When the crash occurred the other boy was not at my side. I do not know what part of the road the motorcyclist was on at the time of the accident. After Bert's bicycle struck me I looked up and saw the motorcycle about five yards in front in the direction in which I was going and the rider going over the handlebars. We had been riding one behind the other for about 100 yards.[8]

On 15 May 1935, two days after the crash, Fletcher had told a reporter from Bournemouth's *Daily Echo* that

The man [Lawrence] who had gone over the handlebars had landed with his feet about 5 yards in front of the motor cycle which was about five yards in front of where I fell.[9]

Fellow cyclist Bert Hargraves, who was also aged fourteen, stated that

Opposite Clouds Hill Camp I was riding four to five feet behind Fletcher and on the left-hand side of the road. I heard the sound of a motorcycle coming from behind. No motor car passed me about this time nor any traffic of any sort. I do not remember any more until I found myself in Hospital.

We were riding at a normal pace with both hands on the handlebars. We changed position because of the noise of the motor-cycle. We had been riding in single file for about eighty yards. When we left Bovington Camp we were riding abreast. I slowed up and got behind Frank. I did not wobble at all.[10]

Money bag carried by Bert Hargraves at the time of the crash. Photo: courtesy of R. A. Hammersely: Wareham Town Museum

Almost five decades later, in 1982, Hargraves stated, 'I was in Wool Military Hospital for eleven days.'[11] However, his mother Agnes, said that her son was in hospital for only nine days.[12]

In early 1985, Fletcher was again interviewed by a reporter from Bournemouth's *Daily Echo*

> You've got the straight bit of road first of all and then it dipped down a bend a wee bit more than up again. The second dip we were above [i.e. beyond] that – a few yards along, he wouldn't have seen us like.[13]

On 18 May 1985, Fletcher, now a resident of Wandsworth, was quoted in Bournemouth's *Daily Echo* as saying

> The motorbike itself skidded along the road – I thought it was going to explode – I straightened myself up and looked round. I saw my mate unconscious. Then I looked across the road. I saw Mr Lawrence go over the handlebars and the bike skid across the road. It wasn't a very wide road, more like a track then, and he was sitting up against a tree facing Bovington Camp. So I went across to him and saw this blood on his face. The next thing I knew the soldiers came and an ambulance, which must have come from the camp…

Fletcher was adamant that at the time of the crash

> Bert was definitely behind me – because he was the one that told me to get to the side of the road in front of me [i.e. to get to the nearside].[14]

Interviewed on 10 February 1986, Joan Hughes née Way, whose family resided in a caravan at Clouds Hill, stated that

> on the day of the accident… she was riding/pushing her bicycle from her home at Clouds Hill, towards Bovington village. (Her sisters were bathing in one of the tanks of the three water towers on the west side of the road opposite Clouds Hill summer camp [i.e. Wool Camp].) She had to get off the bicycle several times as one tyre had punctured. She tried to maintain the air pressure by using the hand pump without success. As she walked she came in sight of the three water towers on her right (west) with the bell tents, etc, on her left (east) at Wool Camp. Just before the water towers were a

number of soldiers in the road. There was a lorry and an Army ambulance which looked like the one that usually stood by the medical tent at Wool Camp. A motorcycle was lying in the road and two cycles, one of which was a delivery cycle from Bovington village.

She stood by the crowd of soldiers as the ambulance door was closed. It was driven off followed by the lorry. A soldier by her said, 'The poor sod, if it hadn't been for those water butts he would have missed that tree.'

The inference is that but for the presence of the water tower/butt nearest to the road on the nearside, Lawrence would have been able to swerve onto the nearside verge and thus avoid the boys. The soldier added that he saw it [the crash] happen. Having left her home at Clouds Hill, at no time did she see any vehicle, car or otherwise, pass her in either direction.[15]

On 13 August 1991, Fletcher stated as follows

So as you go along a bit more there's two more hills, one down and one up, and then you get to your flat road again. Well we must have been on the second hill about 150 yards along the road at the time. When… we heard this motorbike come along. Like Bertie said we had better get inside [i.e. to the nearside of] the road. So we must have [done so] as he [Lawrence] was coming up the road. He must have seen us too late. That's the way I looked at it. And then, uh, he didn't have time to pull out.

Well the next thing I knew, I heard Bertie's bike go down with a wallop as it [Lawrence's Brough] hit the back wheel. He [Lawrence] went over his handlebars before the bike went along there… Over like that, and then the bike skidded straight along the road. That's how I found him sitting up against the tree with blood coming down his face. [As regards the Brough] the wheels was out towards the road and the saddle was in towards the kerb. He went in front a bit and I saw him go over, then the bike came to him and skidded like that there (demonstrates side skidding). The bike fell over afterwards.

From this account, it is not clear whether the Brough came to rest on its right side or its left. However, a subsequent examination of the machine indicated that the principal damage sustained was to its right side.

> As he came out of the dip and onto a straight road he could not possibly have seen us because the hill's that steeper you know. He must have come up and saw us too late along there. And then Bertie's bike caught mine there…. We're on the side of the road. His [Bert's] front wheel just touched my back wheel, that was all.

Subsequently, said Fletcher

> These guys came and they sent for an ambulance. Which presumably is the field ambulance which the camp [Wool Camp] used to have. The two casualties went [were stretchered] into the ambulance and then they went to Bovington Camp.[16]

In their book *A Handful with Quietness*, published in 1992, Lawrence's neighbours Pat and Joyce Knowles stated as follows

> The first person on the scene was… a man who prefers to remain anonymous. He was employed as a lorry driver at the time and with his 'mate' was working about a hundred yards east of the road where the accident took place. They were loading gear and equipment which had been used for a weekend territorial camp.
>
> From where he was standing he saw the motorcycle come down the road into the camp, although at the time he was not aware that it was Shaw. Much later he heard the motorcycle again but didn't turn away from his task.

This account indicates that Lawrence had first paid a visit to Wool Camp, when en route to Bovington.

> Then suddenly, when he heard the engine race, the wheels spinning uselessly, he turned and saw the motorcycle on its side and a figure lying nearby. With his companion he ran

across quickly, and although the injured man's face was covered with blood, he realised from the Brough and the overalls that the man was wearing that it must be Lawrence. In surprise, he said 'Why it's Lawrence,' whereupon Shaw opened his eyes and smiled and raised his hand with one finger extended – a gesture which has caused much speculation. Shaw then went into a coma without saying a word, a coma from which he never regained consciousness.[17]

(Joyce Knowles later revealed that the anonymous person referred to above was her cousin, Lyall Chapman.)[18]

On 13 August 1991, Fletcher described the state of Tank Park Road at the time. It

was a rough sort of road where the tanks used to go along. They used to go on the moors…, then they used to cross this road on to the other moor. It was tar, a kind of tarry, but was rough with the tracks of the tanks.[19]

John B. Conolly, a soldier from Bovington who was ordered to attend the crash site in case extra help was required, said

the piece of road near where the crash accident took place had been resurfaced by the usual method at the time, namely, sprayed with tar and stones simply thrown on the top.[20]

What of the alleged black car, seen by Corporal Catchpole, but evidently by no one else? On 5 September 1985 the following letter was published in Bournemouth's *Daily Echo*.

I can assure you there definitely was a car, and it was a black one. It was a Hillman. The registration number was COW 41, and I know who was driving it. The driver and Lawrence waved at each other as they passed.

The letter was from a Mrs Margaret Montague of Wimborne.[21] In November 1985, Margaret stated that

when Lionel Montague [her husband, who was manager of an

insurance company[22]] arrived in Sandford Garage, north of Wareham, having passed through Wareham, Mr Douglas Hope, the then owner of the garage, or one of his employees, told Montague that Lawrence had had an accident. Montague replied (in the vein of) he didn't believe it as he had just waved to him on the road near Clouds Hill.

The car, said Margaret, was a black 'Hillman 10'.[23]

Eighteen

A Reappraisal
of the Crash

EVER SINCE THE CRASH, controversy has swirled around Lawrence and his state of mind at the time. Did he, in fact, commit suicide? In order to come to a conclusion about this it is, therefore, necessary to reconstruct the circumstances of his final motorcycle ride in more detail.

Manufacturer George Brough examined the motorcycle subsequent to the crash and found no structural or mechanical failure. However, Private Arthur Russell of the Royal Tank Corps, who had collected both the Brough and Hargraves' bicycle from the crash site and taken them to the Inquest, noticed that the front brake cable had snapped – presumably as a result of frantic braking by Lawrence.[1]

Diagrams made of the crash site

In their biography of Lawrence, Paul Marriott and Yvonne Argent included 'Frank Fletcher's sketch map of the crash site on 13 May 1935'.[2] This is not an original sketch, but appears to have been created by the authors from information given to them by Fletcher himself.

In the sketch the accident spot is marked by an asterisk. Hargraves' body is lying on the nearside, near to the crown of the road with his bicycle beside him, also on the nearside. However, the asterisk is just *beyond* Hargraves and his bicycle, implying that both were knocked *backwards* - which is impossible. Fletcher is depicted lying on the nearside, beyond his bicycle which is also on the nearside, and level with the asterisk. As for Lawrence, he is shown on the offside (i.e. east side), lying half on the road and half on the verge, with his head almost touching a tree. On the nearside of the road is the Brough.

In 1986, as a result of his interview with Joan Hughes, author and former RAF officer Roland A. Hammersley, made a sketch of how Joan remembered the site 50 years after the crash. The sketch depicts, on the east side of the road, Wool Camp with its tents, including the medical marquee, and a line of telegraph poles. On the west side are depicted the three water towers, and a tree with damage to its bark. On the road itself, the positions of the ambulance and lorry are shown, and also a skid mark, then a gap, and beyond this, a score mark. Missing from the sketch are the positions, subsequent to the crash, of a) Lawrence's body; b) the Brough, and c) the two boy cyclists and their bicycles.[3]

Both of the above sketches are misleading, in that they give the impression that the road was straight at this point, which is not the case, as will be demonstrated.

The weather

Did weather conditions play a part, in regard to the crash? The evidence is, probably not.

> The morning was part sunshine part cloud, with half the sky covered with cloud at 10 a.m. (clock time) observation. The wind at 9:00 GMT [Greenwich Mean Time] was recorded as NNE Force 4, a moderate breeze. The maximum temperature was 53 degrees Fahrenheit (12 degrees Celcius), minimum temperature was 37 degrees F (3 degrees C). There was 7.9 hours of sunshine during the whole day, and no rain.[4]

Damage to the Brough

In view of the presence of score marks on the road and the damage to Hargraves' bicycle, it is not surprising that there was damage to the Brough. This included: offside footrest broken off; left handlebar bent; right gear-change lever pushed against petrol tank causing indentations; rear brake pedal grazed and bent; kick-start pedal bent upwards; silencer, rear tool boxes, saddle, and mudguards grazed; headlamp rim dislodged. The Brough was discovered to be in second gear, and although it was capable of speeds of 85 mph in this gear,[5] it is possible that the machine was in third (top) gear at the time of the crash, and that the gear-change lever was jogged out of position on impact with the road.

Damage to Hargraves' bicycle

Three photographs taken after the crash[6] revealed severe damage to the rear wheel, part of its frame having been bent into the shape of a U, the

Hargraves's damaged bicycle, being examined by Private Arthur Russell.

apex of which reached as far as the axle; bending of the rear forks, in particular the offside fork forwards and outwards; crumpling of the rear mudguard, and distortion of the spokes. The chain was still in position on its front and rear sprocket wheels, but slack, indicating that the entire rear section of the frame had been shunted forward by the impact, relative to the front.

In order to produce this pattern of damage, the Brough must have struck the bicycle from behind and from the nearside, but at a slight angle rather than straight on. This would have had the effect, not only of producing the observed indentation in the wheel, but also of bending the forks in the manner described. In other words, when viewed from above, the rear wheel would have been forced in an anti-clockwise direction, putting extreme stress on the offside of the rear axle, a stress which was transmitted to the offside fork. This anti-clockwise distortion of the axle (when viewed from above) on which the rear sprocket wheel was mounted also accounts for the slackness of the chain.

This said, the conclusion must be that immediately prior to impact, either a) Hargraves was steering towards the nearside – a natural reaction with a high-powered motorcycle approaching rapidly from behind – or b) that Lawrence was steering slightly towards the offside, in an attempt to avoid him. From the direction of the Brough's skidmark in the Hammersley/Hughes sketch, which is slightly towards the offside direction, the latter appears to have been the case.

A reconstruction of the crash

On the morning of Monday 13 May 1935, T. E. Lawrence is travelling on his motorcycle from Bovington northwards along Tank Park Road, on the return journey towards his cottage, Clouds Hill, a mile or so distant. To begin with, the road is long and fairly straight, as it ascends a gentle gradient, through open heathland. As Lawrence approaches the brow of the hill, the road begins to curve gently to the right. By the time he has reached this point he has travelled approximately 1,400 yards, or just under one mile, at an average speed of 50-60 mph – based on what is known of his motorcycling habits. Meanwhile, two boys Frank Fletcher and Bert Hargraves, are cycling abreast and ahead of him in the same direction. On hearing the roar of the motorcycle they move into single file, with Hargraves at the rear and Fletcher at the front. Even though the Brough was a powerful machine, the bend in the road, together with the presence of the hillock, and the fact that the wind was blowing force 4 (i.e. at about 15 m.p.h.) from north-north-east may have meant that the boys did not hear the motorcycle until the final few seconds before impact.

Beyond the brow, the road commences a long left turn, and descends into a dip before ascending to a second brow. To his right, is the military, tented summer camp. To negotiate this section at speed, Lawrence is obliged to lean inwards to counteract the centrifugal force which is acting on him and his machine. Being familiar with the road, a daredevil such as he, would have found the prospect of zooming up the hill, down the dip, and up again, exhilarating.

Having ascended the second brow, Lawrence and the Brough are almost airborne, when suddenly, immediately in front of him, is Hargraves. By now, according to Fletcher, he and his fellow cyclist had ascended the second brow and were on the downslope. Lawrence slams on his brakes and the tyres leave their mark on the road, but a collision is inevitable, and the Brough's front wheel (which is 21 inches in diameter) impacts with the rear wheel of the errand boy's bicycle (26 inches in diameter). Given the relative speeds at which they were travelling, and their respective weights (excluding their riders), the momentum of the Brough was forty times that of the bicycle.[7] Because of the disparity in size between the impacting wheels, and the fact that the two vehicles were travelling in virtually the same direction, the impact causes the bicycle to be projected into the air in a forward direction, giving credence to Fletcher's assertion that Hargraves' bicycle fell on top of him.

Finally, because the Brough's front wheel struck Hargraves' rear wheel at a slight angle, and not in a straight line, the immense force of the impact would have caused Hargraves' bicycle to spin in an anti-clockwise direction. Both boy cyclists are, not surprisingly, thrown off, but mercifully survive to tell the tale.

On impact, owing to the sudden deceleration of the Brough, Lawrence too is immediately thrown off. His body flies upwards, and the centrifugal force which acts on it by virtue of the bend, causes it to be projected to the right (offside). As his only injuries were allegedly to his head, it is assumed that this impacted heavily, either with the road, or, as seems more likely, with a roadside tree. (A crash helmet might have saved Lawrence's life, but

The damaged Brough. Photo: Jonathan M. Weekly

it was not his custom to wear one.) Meanwhile, the Brough's momentum carries it forwards until it finally topples over onto its side and comes to rest, leaving score marks on the road.

Was there a black car?

Whether or not a black car was travelling along the road from Clouds Hill towards Bovington at the time in question remains a mystery. Corporal Catchpole was adamant that he saw it, and Margaret Montague, as already mentioned, had suggested a likely candidate – i.e. the black 'Hillman 10', which her husband had been driving that very morning on that very road, when he alleged that he saw and exchanged greetings with Lawrence. However, neither boy cyclist saw any such car, and furthermore, according to the evidence of Inspector Drake of the Dorset Constabulary (given at the inquest)

> in consequence of receiving a statement about a motor-car being on the road at the time, inquiries had been made in the district of a number of people. No other person than Cpl Catchpole could say they saw a car, and the Lieutenant in charge of the Camp could not say he saw a car.[8]

Supposing Catchpole was right, and such a car *did* pass Lawrence immediately prior to the crash. Then he would have been obliged to move away from the crown of the road and towards his nearside, which would help to explain why he was unable to avoid a collision with Hargraves' bicycle. Why, therefore, did the owner of the black car not come forward subsequently? Probably because a), he himself had not been involved in any collision and b), he may not even have been aware, at the time, that a road traffic accident had occurred. But it is difficult to believe, in view of the publicity, that news of it did not reach him subsequently.

Is it possible that, for some unknown reason, the driver of the black car was visiting the camp, and having done so, emerged from it and turned left onto Tank Park Road just after the boy cyclists had passed it – hence their failure to observe the vehicle? But if so, how was it possible for the car to achieve a speed of 30 mph in the space of only 20 feet? The likelihood is, therefore, that there was no black car on the road at the time in question.

Nineteen

THE EXACT LOCATION
OF THE CRASH

From the description given by the two boy cyclists Hargraves and Fletcher, and others, it is obvious that the topography of Tank Park Road bears no resemblance to the present-day main road linking Bovington to Clouds Hill, namely King George V Road. Why should this be so?

Evidence from maps and aerial photographs

According to the Ordnance Survey (OS) map of 1901 (revised in 1927[1]), what later became known as Tank Park Road ran north-north-westwards from Bovington Camp towards Clouds Hill in virtually a straight line, with only slight curvature apparent immediately to the south of Clouds Hill. The map also reveals that, in its course towards Clouds Hill, the road ascended a gentle gradient of about 2 degrees.

'Wool Camp' (or Clouds Hill Camp) is designated on the map as an area of approximately 150 acres, situated adjacent to Tank Park Road on its east side, and to the east and south-east of Clouds Hill. Tented summer camps were held here, annually, for soldiers from Bovington who were often joined by personnel (such as Corporal Catchpole) from other units, or from the Territorial Army. Here, under canvas, the men accustomed themselves to life 'in the field'.

A sketch that Lawrence made of Clouds Hill in April 1934 shows Tank Park Road running southwards from the cottage, before curving left (i.e. eastwards) and then, in a more pronounced manner, to the right (westwards), before straightening up and pointing towards Bovington.[2]

An aerial photograph taken by the RAF in 1947 shows Clouds Hill, together with both the War Department fence and the new tank track/fire-guard as indicated by Lawrence in his sketch. There is no evidence of a long, straightish road, as shown on the 1901 OS map, but, instead, a more tortuous track to the immediate east of the newly-constructed King George V Road may be seen. However, the point at which the northern end of this track joins the latter road is not discernable.[3]

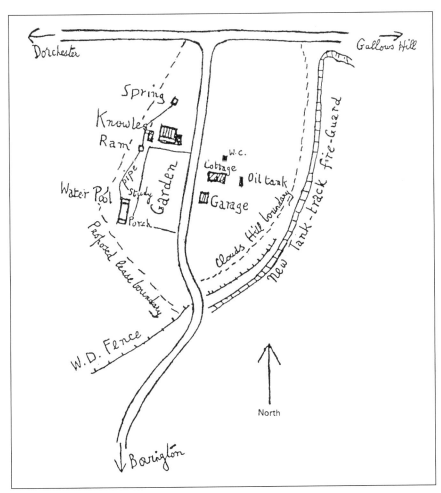

Clouds Hill and its vicinity, sketched by Lawrence, April 1934

On the modern-day Google aerial map of 2008, King George V Road (constructed during the Second World War) is easily identifiable, running in almost a straight line from Bovington to Clouds Hill.[4]

A track running alongside King George V road on its west side may also be seen. However, this track curves considerably more than the road depicted on the 1901 OS map, and is more similar in profile to the RAF map. Finally, this modern-day Google map is far more accurate and informative than maps of yesteryear. It may, therefore, be deduced that the 1901 OS map, as far as what later became known as Tank Park Road is concerned, is a gross over-simplification of the situation on the ground.[5]

Finally, Lawrence's biographer Andrew R. B. Simpson has cleverly super-imposed the position of King George V Road onto the 1901 OS map, thereby demonstrating that this (new) road was constructed almost entirely to the east of Tank Park Road; apart from where the two roads coincide in the immediate vicinity of Clouds Hill cottage.[6]

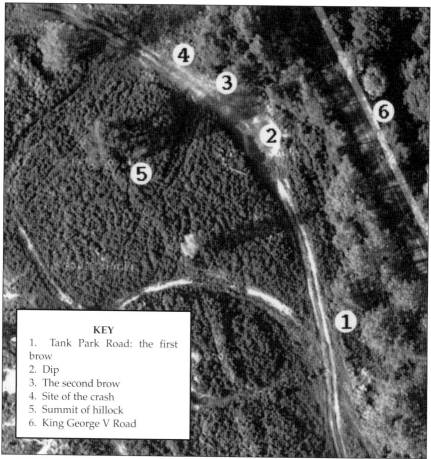

KEY
1. Tank Park Road: the first brow
2. Dip
3. The second brow
4. Site of the crash
5. Summit of hillock
6. King George V Road

Clouds Hill, King George V Road, and remnants of Tank Park Road.
Photo: Google map, 2008

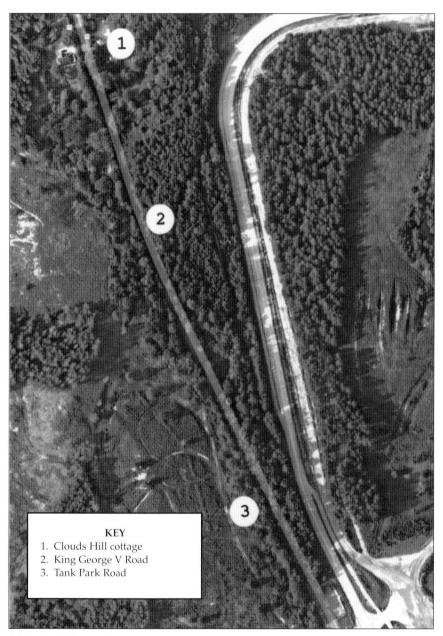

KEY
1. Clouds Hill cottage
2. King George V Road
3. Tank Park Road

Vicinity of the crash. Photo: Google Map 2008

Photographic evidence

In about 1930 a photograph was taken of the first section of Tank Park Road, leading from Bovington towards Clouds Hill.[7] The road is fairly straight, with a slight uphill gradient.

Four further photographs, taken shortly after the crash, are of particular interest.

i) From the crash site, looking southwards towards Bovington one mile or so distant (dated 14 May 1935, the day after the crash, by an unknown photographer).[8] The road, which curves gently to the right (i.e. westwards), ascends to a brow, as seen in the middle distance, then dips, before ascending to another brow. The right-hand (west) side is bordered by an ample covering of trees and bushes; some of the foliage of which overhangs it. On the left (east) side of the road is low scrubland, the occasional tree, and a line of telegraph poles. Incidentally, the water towers/tanks are not visible on this photograph perhaps because a) they were hidden by foliage or b) they were situated immediately to the right of the photographer, and therefore out of view.

ii) From the crash site, looking northwards towards Clouds Hill (dated 14 May 1935, by an unknown photographer, and featuring two motor vehicles).[9] The road begins to bend: first to the left and then more sharply to the right, before straightening up, once again. In the foreground on the left (west) side is a bank, with low scrubland and, in the middle distance, a tree, atop a hillock and set back from the road. The fence marking the boundary of the Moreton Plantation is clearly visible. On the right (east) side, the line of telegraph poles continues northwards. It is possible that the position of the car shown facing north is where the Brough impacted with the bicycle, and the position of the more distant car with its adjacent tree (one of three) is where Lawrence's body came to rest.

iii) From the crash site, taken from the nearside verge of the road looking northwards towards Clouds Hill (mid-May 1935, by Joyce E. Knowles, featuring a single motor vehicle).[10]

Here, the roadside telegraph poles are more clearly visible than in the previous photograph, and the curvature of the road is more clearly demonstrated.

iv) From the crash site, taken from the centre of the road looking northwards (mid-May 1935).[11]

The above photographs indicate that Tank Park Road, with its curves, had an entirely different configuration to King George V Road, which was constructed several years later and is virtually straight. However, if Tank Park Road was simply straightened out to create King George V Road, then one would expect to see remnants of the former road criss-crossing the latter. This is

From crash site looking north, mid-May 1935.
Photo: Joyce E. Knowles

not the case, because the two roads were different entities for virtually their entire lengths – as the 2008 Google map indicates.

Evidence on the ground: the topography of Tank Park Road in 2013

Commencing at a point approximately 1,200 yards from the centre of Bovington, and 660 yards from Clouds Hill cottage, a trackway is identifiable, running northwards alongside King George V Road and, to begin with, within 30-50 yards of it on its west side. This track ascends a gentle slope of about five degrees, curving to the right at first and then more sharply to the left, as it skirts a hillock situated on its west side. At a distance of about 470 yards from Clouds Hill, a brow is reached. Forty-five yards, or so, beyond this brow is a dip 13 feet in depth. Twenty-four yards beyond the dip is a second, smaller brow, which is 4 feet higher than the lowest part of the dip. Then, still curving towards the left, the road begins a long, gentle descent of about 3 degrees, before subsequently curving right towards Clouds Hill, though this final section of the track is much overgrown, and therefore difficult to identify.

Finally, an inch or so beneath the surface of the trackway is a blackish layer about an inch thick and presumably tar, below which is a layer of flintstones – presumably the foundation of the road.

The present-day view of this trackway, from just beyond the second brow, looking both northwards and southwards, bears a striking resemblance to the photographs taken from the crash site in May 1935. It is therefore certain, beyond reasonable doubt, that this was the very place where the crash occurred – i.e. about 20 yards north of the second brow,[12]

The tree in question

In the photograph 'From the crash site looking north', dated 14 May 1935 and featuring the two cars, three trees are visible at the point where the road begins to bend back towards Clouds Hill. Comparing this with the present-day topography of the site, is it possible to identify the likely location for the tree nearest to the road? Yes, and not only that, just where one would expect it – i.e. about 44 yards northwards from the crest of the second brow – are the decayed remnants of the stump of a large tree, presumably a Scots pine.

Given the fact that such trees grow in circumference at the rate of approximately 1 inch per year, and that this tree is estimated (because of its advanced state of decomposition) to have been cut down about 30 years ago, then it is calculated that in 1935, its trunk would have been about 2 feet in diameter. So perhaps this is indeed the tree in question, the one adjacent to which Lawrence's body came to rest, and with which his head probably impacted.

The author and the tree stump in question, October 2013

Finally, from the photographs it is clear that the carriageway was more than wide enough for two vehicles to pass abreast of one other. So, had Lawrence been travelling at a speed more appropriate for the road conditions, he would have had no difficulty in overtaking the two cyclists, as Corporal Catchpole pointed out.

The evidence indicates that the crash was an accident, and no more. The 'suicide theory' may therefore be dispensed with a) for this reason; b) because Lawrence's mood was, in the main, buoyant, as he commenced his retirement; c) he sent a telegram to Williamson inviting him to Clouds Hill the following day – an event which he was no doubt looking forward to.

Ultimately, if Lawrence had indeed intended to commit suicide, it is hardly likely that he would have left letters of a sensitive and confidential nature lying about in the cottage for anyone to find after his death.

Twenty

THE FUNERAL:
AFTERMATH

L AWRENCE'S FUNERAL was held on the afternoon of 21 May 1935 at the Church of St Nicholas, Moreton. Canon Michael W. Kinlock, the rector, officiated. Psalm CXXI, 'I will lift up mine eyes unto the hills: from whence cometh my help', was sung, together with the hymn commencing 'Jesu, Lover of my soul'.

Mourners – of whom there were many – included Florence Hardy; Mr and Mrs Winston Churchill; Augustus John; Lady Astor; Mr and Mrs Siegfried

Lawrence's funeral procession, 21 May 1935.
Photo: Wareham Town Museum

The funeral: Winston Churchill, his wife Clementine on his left, and second from his right, Bert Hargraves. Photo: Wareham Town Museum

The coffin thronged by mourners. Photo: Jonathan M. Weekly

Sassoon; Aircraftman Bradbury of the RAF; and Private Russell of the Royal Tank Corps. Also present were representatives of the King of Iraq, and of the Emir Abdullah of Transjordan.

The Shaws were absent (on a cruise to South Africa); as was E. M. Forster, who later visited Clouds Hill with the Sassoons. Neither Trenchard nor Allenby, nor Robert Graves attended. Feisal had died in Switzerland two years earlier, and there was no representative of Lawrence's late father's family, the Chapmans. His brother Arnold was present, but not his mother Sarah, nor his brother Bob, who were on their way home from China and did not yet know of his death.

John Bruce, having learned of Lawrence's motorcycle crash, stated as follows

> I stayed in Bournemouth while waiting for his death to come. I stayed on at my hotel, until the day of the funeral which was Tuesday, the twenty-first. I went to the cottage, waited outside till the cortege came, and followed him to his last resting place.[1]

The same day, a message from King George V to Arnold Lawrence was published in *The Times* newspaper.

The King has heard with sincere regret of the death of your brother, and deeply sympathises with you and your family at this sad loss. Your brother's name will live in history, and the King gratefully recognizes his distinguished services to his country and feels that it is tragic that the end should have come in this manner to a life still so full of promise.

Lawrence was buried in Moreton cemetery in a plot immediately adjacent to that of his dear friends and neighbours, W. Arthur Knowles and his wife Henrietta.

The inscription on Lawrence's tombstone (the grave was originally marked simply by a wooden cross), erected by his mother, reads as follows

TO THE DEAR MEMORY OF
T. E. LAWRENCE
FELLOW OF ALL SOVLS COLLEGE
OXFORD
BORN 16 AVGVST 1888
DIED 19 MAY 1935
THE HOVR IS COMING & NOW IS
WHEN THE DEAD SHALL HEAR
THE VOICE OF THE
SON OF GOD
AND THEY THAT HEAR
SHALL LIVE

The Roses

Lawrence's grave. Photo: courtesy of the Rector of Moreton

In May 1985 a mysterious note appeared on the grave, which read: 'I have kept the secret still.' What could this secret have been?

For many years, on the anniversary of Lawrence's birthday (16 August), a bouquet of white roses was delivered to the Rector of Moreton, to be placed on Lawrence's grave. (The company Interflora, which delivered the flowers, confirmed that the order for them came from the U.S.A.) The order also stipulated that on the same date, a single white rose was to be delivered to Lawrence's cottage, Clouds Hill.[2] Furthermore, each year, the bouquet contained one less rose. For example, in 1984 there were 36 roses and by 1993, the number had fallen to 27. In that year, 1993, an intriguing message accompanied the roses. It read, 'In memory of T.E.S. 2020 AD', 2020 being the year following 2019, when the final rose was due to be delivered. Incidentally, another flower, a geranium, was also placed on Lawrence's grave annually; also from an anonymous donor.

Lawrence's grave, with roses and note.
Photo: Wareham Town Museum

What was 'the secret', mentioned in the mysterious note placed on Lawrence's grave in 1985, and what is the significance of the date '2020'? And are the two related in any way. Perhaps in that year, all will be revealed!

On 18 August 1994, the following article by Thomas J. Brady, entitled 'Lawrence of Arabia and the Lure of the Roses', was published online.

> A mysterious bouquet of white roses, laid on British war hero Lawrence of Arabia's grave each year since he died in 1935, failed to appear on Tuesday. The flowers had been ordered annually on his birthday, Aug. 16, by a U.S. admirer whose identity has never been revealed and who may have died or fallen ill. 'It appears the order has not been placed in America, which is very sad,' said Rosemary Wise, one of two local florists who used to place the bouquet on the grave at the English village of Moreton.[3]

Twenty One

ERIC HENRI KENNINGTON:
THE LAWRENCE EFFIGY

Eric Henri Kennington.
Photo: London Transport Museum

ERIC KENNINGTON explained how he had been commissioned by Lawrence's brother Arnold, to sculpt a life-sized effigy of Lawrence in his memory.

The shock of T. E.'s death, yes, when we were getting over it I had a letter from Buxton [Robin Buxton, Lawrence's banker and former comrade-in-arms in Arabia] asking me to attend a committee meeting which would plan a national memorial. We met. I attended. As far as I can remember the other members were Buxton in the chair, Lady Astor who soon elbowed him out of it and was in it herself, Newcombe [Captain S. F. Newcombe of the Royal Engineers and formerly director of the Sinai survey], Storrs [Sir Ronald Storrs, formerly assistant to the British High Commissioner in Cairo], Lionel Curtis [administrator and political theorist who popularised the idea of a common-wealth of self-governing nations], Bernard Shaw, Sir Herbert Baker [architect, who had provided Lawrence with the attic room in Barton Street, Westminster where he had written much of *Seven Pillars*]. They said we should make a national appeal. Then Baker said he had asked T. E. once what his idea was for a monument to himself and his reply, 'the largest mountain in Arabia carved into a likeness of himself.'

I lay low till Baker said, 'What about an effigy. We have a distinguished sculptor here.' That was the only meeting I attended but I was told my drawings had been accepted and I was to go ahead and await official confirmation.

Next I wrote to A. W. Lawrence who can be spiteful and vindictive. He came and saw the effigy. 'What's this worth to you,' he said. My answer was, 'Two thousand pounds.' He pulled out a chequebook and wrote out a cheque for two thousand pounds [saying] 'Now its mine and I can do what I like with it.'

We went to Salisbury (cathedral) and looked at the site and met the Dean. He was against it. He said he wanted it in the south transept on a high table tomb. A. W. explained to him, elaborately and architecturally, that this was an effigy in the Early English style, and flattish for putting on a low base, not like the fifteenth-century figures, all knobbly and sticking up so you could see them from below. Of course he was right, but the Dean thought the height of the building demanded a tall base with a raised up figure. Then we went and saw the Bishop at the palace. A. W. wasn't giving in, nor was the Dean (terrible fellow). So having slain a bishop, murdered a dean, turned down a cathedral, A. W., quite ruthless, said, 'We'll go to Wareham.' We fairly danced and said, 'This is the place – St Martin's, Wareham. Then back to Salisbury to tell the Bishop. He was a bit surprised to see us back so soon. He was delighted and said, 'I've always loved that church and from the first I thought it was the right place for the Lawrence effigy.'[1]

Pat Knowles, however, begged to differ and stated that it was *he* who had suggested Wareham's tenth century church of St Martin's-on-the-Walls.

> It is my proud claim to have introduced Kennington to the site while showing him around Dorset seeking likely places for the statue. When Kennington walked into the church he said emphatically 'this is it!'[2]

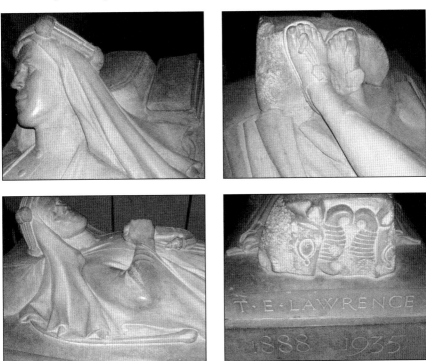

The effigy was created by Kennington in his studio at Homer House near Reading, Berkshire. Wing Commander Reginald G. Sims (with whom Lawrence had worked at Bridlington and who was an expert amateur photographer) photographed the sculpture at its various stages of development. Said Kennington, 'The photos are welcome. I profit by these. They show me errors.' Undoubtedly it was this help from Sims which enabled Kennington to produce the exquisite likeness of Lawrence which he achieved.[3]

Richard Knowles (formerly of RAF Cattewater, Plymouth) gave an excellent description of the effigy, which was carved from a 3-ton block of Portland stone.

> Lawrence is represented in his Arab robes and headdress from the fabled period of his involvement with the Arab Revolt during the First World War. The right hand rests on the hilt of his dagger whilst the left lies loosely at his side. His feet rest upon a piece of Hittite sculpture representing his pre-war archaeological days at Carchemish, his head lies on a camel saddle and beside it are three unlabelled books which represent those that he always carried with him, including on the Arab campaign – Morte d'Arthur, the Oxford Book of English Verse, and a Greek Anthology. The chest upon which the effigy lies carries only the simple text 'T E Lawrence 1888 1935'. The effigy is in an unashamed English fourteenth-century style with crossed legs, the Arab robes being treated rather as the medieval gown.[4]

The effigy was installed in the church during the first week of September 1939, having spent the previous night in the rectory garden. It had taken its creator Kennington, three years to complete.

Epilogue

L AWRENCE, IN HIS TIME, had gazed in awe at the wonders of Western Europe and the Middle East; in *Seven Pillars*, he had described the 'stupendous' mountains of Wadi Rum in southern present-day Jordan. And yet, to him, Clouds Hill was his 'earthly paradise'.

In 1936, his brother Arnold, donated the property to the National Trust and Joyce Knowles became its caretaker and curator: a role which she fulfilled for more than fifty years.

Had it not been for Winston Churchill, Clouds Hill would no longer exist. The reason for this was given by E. V. G. Hunt. During the Second World War

Joyce Knowles at Clouds Hill, with A. Norman MacConnell, representative of the RAF Marine Branch Association. Photo: Wareham Town Museum

the war department planned road widening at Cloud's Hill which would have taken the [the army's tanks] within feet of the cottage. The vibrations from passing tanks would have made short work of the foundations. Pat [Knowles] wrote to the National Trust but they were powerless to do anything. Pat wouldn't take that as the final word.... He sent a telegram to Winston Churchill who in turn sent a telegram to the M. O. D. (Ministry of Defence) stopping all work until further orders. Pat was invited to give an alternative plan for the road, which he did – and which was accepted with the result that Clouds Hill was saved.[1]

Lawrence's mother Sarah, having returned from China settled in Swanage, Dorset, where she died in 1959, aged ninety-eight. She lies in in Wolvercote

Cemetery, Oxford, where her husband Thomas Tighe Chapman, who died on 8 April 1919, is also buried.

Lawrence's eldest brother Bob, died in 1971. His youngest brother Arnold, who was the only one of the five to marry, became Professor of Classical Archaeology at Cambridge and lived, for some years, in Ghana, where he established a museum. He died on Easter Sunday 1991 aged ninety years.

At rest in Moreton Cemetery, Lawrence is in the company of some of those whom he held most dear. In the grave immediately adjacent to his lie (William) Arthur Knowles and his wife Henrietta. The grave also includes a memorial to their son Bill, who lost his life on 10 May 1940 whilst on active service with the RAF. Elsewhere in the cemetery lie Pat Knowles (died 30 May 1981, aged seventy-four) and his wife Joyce (died 28 March 1998, aged eighty-eight).

Pat Knowles at his family home. Photo: Robert Hunt

Also in the same cemetery were interred Thomas W. Beaumont (died 29 August 1991, aged ninety-three, who had served with Lawrence in the desert in the Machine Gun Corps) and his wife Helen (died 5 March 2006); Canon Michael W. Kinlock, Rector of St Nicholas Church, Moreton; and finally, Lawrence's kinsman Henry R. Fetherstonhaugh Frampton of Moreton (died 8 January 1955, aged ninety-five).

Thomas W. Beaumont planting a tree beside King George V Road in memory of Lawrence, on 13 May 1983, the 48th anniversary of the crash. Photo: Wareham Town Museum

Lawrence's funeral bier. Photo: Moreton Tea Rooms

The character of T. E. Lawrence was a complex one, of this there is no doubt: masochism and Sexual Aversion Disorder being part of his inherent make-up, but it was the mental trauma that he suffered, following his rape by the Turks, which brought him low and almost destroyed him.

In Lawrence's day rape was a taboo subject. However, one would like to think that had he lived in the modern world, he would have been recognized as suffering from Post-Rape-Trauma Syndrome, and been offered the appropriate advice and support which he so desperately required. And yet, despite all, he retained his sense of humour, and it would doubtless have amused him to learn that the bier on which his coffin had rested would subsequently serve a useful purpose as a cake stand at the Moreton Tea Rooms – formerly Moreton School!

At Clouds Hill, his beloved Dorsetshire cottage, with favourite music provided by his gramophone, and in the company of his neighbours the Knowles, servicemen colleagues, and his literary and artistic friends, his spirits were restored. Now, full of hope and joyful anticipation, he could look forward to retirement. But alas, this was to be all too short.

The Lawrence effigy.   Photo: courtesy of the Rector and Churchwardens, church of St Martin's-on-the-walls, Wareham

And so, the abiding image remains of sunshine, streaming in through the stained-glass window of St Martin's-on-the-Walls Church, Wareham, lighting up the effigy of a man who, once so tortured and tormented, is at last, serene and at peace.

APPENDIX 1

Clouds Hill cottage

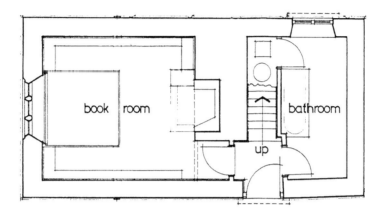

Ground Floor Plan

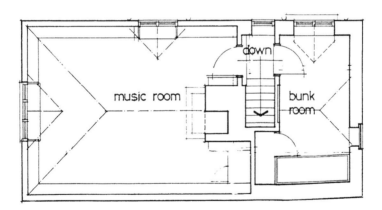

First Floor Plan

APPENDIX 2

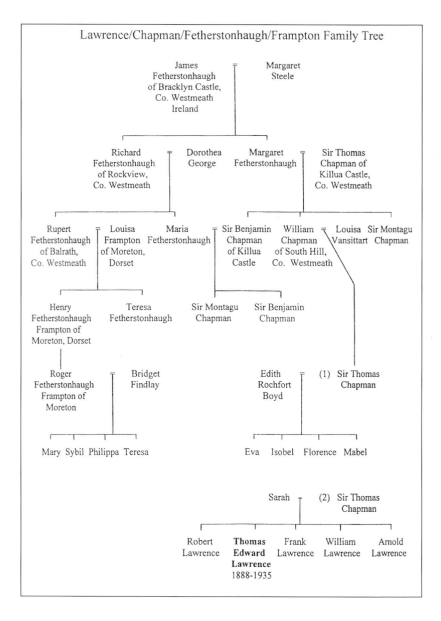

Lawrence/Chapman/Fetherstonhaugh/Frampton Family Tree

James
Fetherstonhaugh
of Bracklyn Castle,
Co. Westmeath
Ireland

Margaret
Steele

Richard
Fetherstonhaugh
of Rockview,
Co. Westmeath

Dorothea
George

Margaret
Fetherstonhaugh

Sir Thomas
Chapman of
Killua Castle,
Co. Westmeath

Rupert
Fetherstonhaugh
of Balrath,
Co. Westmeath

Louisa
Frampton
of Moreton,
Dorset

Maria
Fetherstonhaugh

Sir Benjamin
Chapman
of Killua
Castle

William
Chapman
of South Hill,
Co. Westmeath

Louisa
Vansittart

Sir Montagu
Chapman

Henry
Fetherstonhaugh
Frampton of
Moreton, Dorset

Teresa
Fetherstonhaugh

Sir Montagu
Chapman

Sir Benjamin
Chapman

Roger
Fetherstonhaugh
Frampton of
Moreton

Bridget
Findlay

Edith
Rochfort
Boyd

(1) Sir Thomas
Chapman

Mary Sybil Philippa Teresa

Eva Isobel Florence Mabel

Sarah

(2) Sir Thomas
Chapman

Robert
Lawrence

**Thomas
Edward
Lawrence
1888-1935**

Frank
Lawrence

William
Lawrence

Arnold
Lawrence

112

NOTES

Chapter 1   Clouds Hill, and Lawrence's First Sight of it

1. *Seven Pillars of Wisdom* was published in 1922 - 8 copies only, the so-called 'Oxford Text'. This was followed by a so-called 'Subscribers Edition' of 200 or so copies in late 1926.
2. Recollections of Lesley Edward Gates, in Simpson, Andrew R. B., *Another Life: Lawrence After Arabia*, pp.39-40.
3. Bill and Dick Knowles both joined the RAF.
4. Knowles, Patrick and Joyce, and Bob Hunt, *A Handful with Quietness*, p.24.
5. Ibid, p.26
6. This is believed to be the tree which Lawrence was obliged to blow up with gelignite, owing to its size and close proximity to the cottage. Knowles, Patrick and Joyce, op. cit., p.39. The explosion smashed the window of the roof's skylight.
7. Knowles, Patrick and Joyce and Bob Hunt, op. cit., p.20.
8. Ibid, pp.26-7
9. Garnett, David (editor), *The Letters of T. E. Lawrence*, p.435. Three years later, in 1926, Lawrence purchased the freehold of Clouds Hill from his kinsman Henry Fethertonhaugh Frampton of Moreton, for the sum on £450.
10. Knowles, Patrick and Joyce, and Bob Hunt, op. cit: E. V. G. Hunt: 'Pat Knowles of Clouds Hill', p.51.
11. Garnett, David (editor), op. cit., to D. G. Hogarth, 7 July 1927.
12. Brown, Malcolm (editor), *The Letters of T. E. Lawrence*, to Sydney Cockerell, 27 May 1927. The dagger was purchased by his friend Lionel Curtis, and now resides in All Souls College, Oxford.
13. Knowles, Patrick and Joyce, and Bob Hunt, op. cit., p.27.
14. Saudi Arabia from 1932. These doors are now in Oxford's Ashmolean Museum.
15. Legg, Rodney, *Lawrence in Dorset*, pp.70,75.
16. Brown, Malcolm (editor), op. cit., to Charlotte Shaw, 10 June 1924.
17. Ibid, to Charlotte Shaw, 31 September 1924.
18. Ibid, to E. M. Forster, 17 June 1925.

Chapter 2   Lawrence Sheds his Former Image and Identity: The Armed Services

1. Garnett, David (editor), *The Letters of T. E. Lawrence*, to Dr Hogarth, 13 June 1923.
2. Churchill, Winston, *Lawrence of Arabia as I Knew Him*.

3. Lawrence, A. W. (editor), *Letters to T. E. Lawrence*, from King Feisal I of Iraq, 18 December 1932.

4. Lawrence, A. W. (editor), *T. E. Lawrence by His Friends*, p.120.

5. Ibid, p.221.

6. Smith, Clare Sydney, *The Golden Reign*, pp.36-7.

7. Brown, Malcolm and Julia Cave, *A Touch of Genius: The Life of T. E. Lawrence*, p.176, Note 1.

8. University of Texas Counselling and Mental Health Center and Wisconsin Coalition Against Sexual Assault, Dr Michael Hunter, Ph.D. Article, 'The Disputed Sexuality of T. E. Lawrence', in First World War.com. 1 December 2002.

9. Lawrence, A. W. (editor), *T. E. Lawrence by His Friends*, p.282.

Chapter 3.   Everyday Life at Clouds Hill

1. Garnett, David (editor), *The Letters of T. E. Lawrence*, to Lorna Norrington, 24 February 1935.

2. Knowles, Patrick and Joyce, and Bob Hunt, *A Handful with Quietness*, p.103.

3. Ibid, p.27.

4. Ibid, p.28.

5. Ibid, p.27.

6. *Clouds Hill*, The National Trust, p.6.

7. Ibid, p.11.

8. Ibid, p.11.

9. Smith, Clare Sydney, *The Golden Reign*, p.155.

10. Ibid, pp.60-1.

11. Lawrence, A. W. (editor), *T. E. Lawrence by His Friends*, Jonathan Cape, 1937, 'Gramophone records at Clouds Hill', pp.523-529.

12. Clouds Hill, Dorset, op. cit., p.4.

13. Clouds Hill, Dorset, op. cit., p.11.

14. Lawrence, A. W. (editor), op. cit., pp.63-4.

15. Ibid, p.248.

16. Forster, E. M. 'Clouds Hill', *The Listener*, 1 September 1938, p.426.

17. Knowles, Patrick and Joyce, and Bob Hunt, op. cit., p.38.

18. Brown, Malcolm (editor), *The Letters of T. E. Lawrence*, to Mrs Thomas Hardy, 31 January 1924.

19. *T. E. Lawrence Papers*, Bodleian Library, Oxford, to Sir Ernest M. Dowson, undated.

Chapter 4.   His Books: His Mastery of Foreign Languages

1. Garnett, David (editor), *The Letters of T. E. Lawrence*, to R. V. Buxton, 26 March 1925.

2. Lawrence, A. W. (editor), *T. E. Lawrence by His Friends*, p.21.

3. Soanes, Catherine and Angus Stevenson (editors), *Oxford Dictionary of English*.
4. Liddell Hart, Basil, *T. E. Lawrence to his Biographer*, p.50.
5. Lawrence, A. W. (editor), op. cit., p. 23.
6. Ibid, p.47.
7. Ibid, p.389
8. Garnett, David (editor), op. cit., to C. Day Lewis, 20 December 1934.
9. Lawrence, A. W. (editor), op. cit., p.66
10. Ibid, p.207.
11. Smith, Clare Sydney, *The Golden Reign*, p.60.

Chapter 5 John Bruce: Lawrence Attempted Suicide

1. Bruce, John, 'Papers Relating to the Medical History of T. E. Lawrence', Misc 196 (2904), courtesy of the Imperial War Museum.
2. Mack, John E., *A Prince of Our Disorder: The Life of T. E. Lawrence*, p.431.
3. Ibid, p.431.
4. Ibid, p.433.

Chapter 6 Lawrence's Sexuality: how can his Masochistic Tendencies be Explained?

1. Brown, Malcolm (editor), *The Letters of T. E. Lawrence*, to E. M. Forster, 21 December 1927.
2. Ibid, to Robert Graves, 6 November 1928.
3. Ibid, to F. L. Lucas, 26 March 1929.
4. Ibid, to Ernest Thurtle, 1 April 1929.
5. Lawrence, T. E. to Ernest Altounyan, 28 December 1933, Bodleian Reserve Manuscripts, d49.
6. Lawrence, T. E., *The Mint*, p.129.
7. Mack, John E., *A Prince of Our Disorder: The Life of T. E. Lawrence*, p.67.
8. *Diagnostic and Statistical Manual of Mental Disorders*, American Psychiatric Association, pp. 541-2.
9. Lawrence, A. W. (editor), *T. E. Lawrence by His Friends*, p.278.
10. Ibid, p.364.
11. Wikipedia - phobia.
12. The word 'masochism' was invented by Austrian psychiatrist Richard F. von Krafft-Ebing (1840-1902), after writer, journalist, and fellow countryman Leopold von Sacher-Masoch, who wrote about masochism, and was a masochist himself.
13. Oxford Dictionaries online.
14. Lawrence, T. E., *Seven Pillars of Wisdom*, p.446.
15. Oxford Dictionaries online.
16. Mack, John E., op. cit., p.433. Bruce also told Mack that, in his opinion, Lawrence was not homosexual.
17. *Diagnostic and Statistical Manual of Mental Disorders*, op. cit., p.573.

18. John E Mack, interview with Arnold Lawrence, 21 July 1968, in Mack, John E., op. cit., p.33.
19. Brown, Malcolm, op. cit., to Charlotte Shaw, 14 April 1927.
20. Lawrence, T. E., *The Mint*, p.42.
21. *Diagnostic and Statistical Manual of Mental Disorders*, op. cit., p.573.
22. The concept of 'sexual script' was created by sociologists John H. Gagnon and William Simon. Viz. their book *Sexual Conduct: The Social Sources of Human Sexuality*, published in 1973.

Chapter 7 Post-Rape-Trauma Syndrome: Rape as a Weapon of War

1. Groth, A. Nicholas and Ann W. Burgess, 'Male Rape: Offenders and Victims', *American Journal of Psychiatry*, 137:7, pp.806-810, 1980.
2. Brown, Malcolm (editor), *The Letters of T. E. Lawrence*, to Deputy Chief Political Officer, Cairo, 28 June 1919.
3. Oxford Dictionaries online.
4. Walker, Jayne, John Archer and Michelle Davies, 'Effects of Male Rape on Psychological Functioning', *British Journal of Clinical Psychology* (2005), 44, pp.445–51.
5. Hart-Davis, Rupert (editor), *Siegfried Sassoon Diaries*, March 1924.
6. Brown, Malcolm (editor), op. cit., to E. M. Forster, 21 December 1927.
7. McMullen, Richie J., *Male Rape*, p.65.
8. Godl, John, 'The Disputed Sexuality of T. E. Lawrence', 22 August 2009, first-worldwar.com.

Chapter 8 Thomas and Florence Hardy: Nellie Titterington

1. Garnett, David (editor), *The Letters of T. E. Lawrence*, to William Rothenstein, 14 April 1928.
2. Legg, Rodney, *Lawrence in Dorset*, Florence Hardy to Robert Graves, 13 June 1927, p.57.
3. Garnett, David (editor), op. cit., pp.460-1.
4. Titterington, Ellen E., *The Domestic Life of Thomas Hardy*.
5. Garnett, David (editor), op. cit., to Mrs Thomas Hardy, 5 May 1927.
6. Ibid, to Mrs Thomas Hardy, 16 April 1928.

Chapter 9 Ou ϕpovtis – 'Why Worry?'

1. Information kindly supplied by Professor Sylvan Bérond.
2. Garnett, David (editor), *The Letters of T. E. Lawrence*, to Mrs Eric Kennington, 18 October 1932.
3. Knowles, Patrick and Joyce, and Bob Hunt, *A Handful with Quietness*, p.36.
4. Lawrence, T. E., *Seven Pillars of Wisdom*, p.502.
5. Brown, Malcolm and Julia Cave, *A Touch of Genius: The Life of T. E. Lawrence*, pp.86-8.

6. Lawrence, A. W. (editor), *T. E. Lawrence by His Friends,* p.207.
7. Ibid, p.56.
8. Lawrence, A. W. (editor), *Oriental Assembly by T. E. Lawrence,* pp.108-9.
9. Ibid, p.112.
10. Ibid, pp.112-3.
11. Ibid, pp.114-5.
12. Ibid, pp.117-8.
13. Lawrence, A. W. (editor), *T. E. Lawrence by His Friends,* p.207.
14. Lawrence, T. E., *Seven Pillars of Wisdom,* p.562.
15. Brown, Malcolm (editor), *The Letters of T. E. Lawrence,* to his mother, 24 June 1911.
16. Knightley, Phillip, and Colin Simpson, *The Secret Lives of Lawrence of Arabia,* pp.188-9.
17. Lawrence, T. E., *Seven Pillars of Wisdom,* pp.441-7.
18. Mack, John E., *A Prince of Our Disorder: The Life of T. E. Lawrence,* p.232.

Chapter 10 A Return to the RAF

1. Brown, Malcolm (editor), *The Letters of T. E. Lawrence,* to Mrs Thomas Hardy, 26 August 1925.
2. *T. E. Lawrence Papers,* Bodleian Library, Oxford, to Dick Knowles, 19 April 1928.
3. Lawrence, A. W. (editor), *T. E. Lawrence by His Friends,* p.266.
4. Smith, Clare Sydney, *The Golden Reign,* p.35.
5. Ibid, p.20.
6. To Lionel Curtis on 28 March 1929, in Wilson, Jeremy, 'T. E. Lawrence at Clouds Hill', *Journal of the T. E. Lawrence Society,* vol III, no.1, Summer 1993, p.51.

Chapter 11 Books: Lawrence's Own Desire to become a Writer or Poet

1. Garnett, David (editor), *The Letters of T. E. Lawrence,* p.753.
2. Lawrence, A. W. (editor), *T. E. Lawrence by His Friends,* Jonathan Cape, 1937, 'Books at Clouds Hill', pp.476-522.
3. Brown, Malcolm (editor), *The Letters of T. E. Lawrence,* to Bernard Shaw, 27 December 1922.
4. Dunbar, Janet, *Mrs G.B.S.: A Biographical Portrait,* pp.266-7, Charlotte Shaw to T. E. Lawrence, 31 December 1922.
5. Garnett, David (editor), op. cit., to D. G. Hogarth, 23 August 1923.
6. Churchill, Winston, *Lawrence of Arabia as I Knew Him.*
7. Brown, Malcolm (editor), op. cit., to E. M. Forster, 20 February 1924.
8. Ibid, to E. M. Forster, 6 April 1924.
9. Lawrence, A. W. (editor), op. cit., pp.367-8.
10. Brown, Malcolm (editor), op. cit., to Charlotte Shaw, 18 August 1927.
11. Garnett, David (editor), op. cit., to Eric Kennington, 16 June 1927.
12. Lawrence, A. W. (editor), op. cit., pp.273-4
13. Brown, Malcolm (editor), op. cit., to Robert Graves, 4 February 1935.

Chapter 12 His Mother Sarah and Brother Bob Come to Stay

1. Knowles, Patrick and Joyce, and Bob Hunt, *A Handful with Quietness,* p.30.
2. Ibid, p.36.
3. *T. E. Lawrence Papers,* Bodleian Library, Oxford, to F. E. Hardy, 24 October 1930.
4. Garnett, David (editor), *The Letters of T. E. Lawrence,* to W. A. Knowles 22 November 1930.
4. Smith, Clare Sydney, *The Golden Reign,* p.125.
5. Brown, Malcolm (editor), *The Letters of T. E. Lawrence,* to Charlotte Shaw, 17 June 1926.
6. Brown, Malcolm and Julia Cave, *A Touch of Genius: The Life of T. E. Lawrence,* to Lady Astor, p.195.

Chapter 13 Other Visitors to Clouds Hill

1. Brown, Malcolm (editor), *The Letters of T. E. Lawrence,* to A. E. 'Jock' Chambers, 27 April 1929.
2. Garnett, David (editor), *The Letters of T. E. Lawrence,* to Bernard Shaw, 20 December 1923.
3. Ibid, *to A. E. Chambers, 26 January 1935.*
4. Information supplied by Jeremy Wilson.
5. Forster, E. M., *Selected Letters of E. M. Forster,* Volume 2, p.50.
6. Brown, Malcolm (editor), op. cit., to E. M. Forster, 6 April 1924.
7. Spencer, Gilbert RA, *Memoirs of a Painter,* p.81.
8. *T. E. Lawrence Papers,* Bodleian Library, Oxford, to Private Palmer, 15 March 1927. 'Insha Allah – Arabic for 'God willing'.

Chapter 14 Further Improvements to the Cottage

1. Brown, Malcolm (editor), *The Letters of T. E. Lawrence,* to A.E. (Jock) Chambers, 29 April 1919.
2. *T. E. Lawrence Papers,* Bodleian Library, Oxford, to R. V. Buxton, 5 October 1930.
3. Garnett, David (editor), *The Letters of T. E. Lawrence,* to W.A. Knowles, 10 February 1930.
4. Ibid, to W. A. Knowles 22 November 1930.
5. *T. E. Lawrence Papers,* op. cit., to Charlotte Shaw, 24 November 1931.
6. Garnett, David (editor), op. cit., to G. W. M. Dunn, 9 November 1932.
7. Brown, Malcolm (editor), op. cit., to Mrs Thomas Hardy, 3 December 1932.
8. Knowles, Patrick and Joyce, and Bob Hunt, *A Handful with Quietness,* pp.30-1.
9. Ibid, p.32.
10. Ibid, pp.34-5.
11. Ibid, p.32.
12. Garnett, David (editor), op. cit., to Mrs Thomas Hardy, 25 April 1933.
13. Ibid, to R. G. Goslett, 31 August 1933.

14. Brown, Malcolm (editor), op. cit., to Mrs Charlotte Shaw, 31 August 1933.
15. Lawrence, A. W., *The Home Letters of T. E. Lawrence and his Brothers*, to his mother, 25 September 1933.
16. *T. E. Lawrence Papers*, op. cit., to Charlotte Shaw, 3 October 1933.
17. Information kindly provided by Jeremy Wilson.
18. Brown, Malcolm (editor), op. cit., to Lady Astor, 11 December 1933.
19. When Lawrence died, his estate including Clouds Hill and its land was valued at £7,441 gross, of which investments totalled £2,576. Orlans, Harold, *Biography of a Broken Hero*, p.133.
20. Garnett, David (editor), op. cit., to W. E. Jeffrey, 21 December 1933.
21. Brown, Malcolm (editor), op. cit., to Alec Dixon, 21 December 1933.
22. *T. E. Lawrence Papers*, op. cit., to T. B. Marson, 21 December 1933.
23. Garnett, David (editor), op. cit., to A. W. Lawrence, 26 December 1933.
24. Ibid, to Lady Astor, 31 December 1933.
25. Ibid, p.791
26. Lawrence, M. R. (editor), *The Home Letters of T.E. Lawrence and his Brothers*, to his mother, 6 April 1934.
27. Garnett, David (editor), op. cit., to E. M. Forster 26 June 1934.
28. Brown, Malcolm (editor), op. cit., to Lady Astor, 27 July 1934.
29. Ibid, to Frederic Manning, 16 November 1934.
30. Garnett, David (editor), op. cit., p.830.
31. Brown, Malcolm (editor), op. cit., to Hon. Francis Rodd, 23 November 1934.
32. Ibid, to Mrs Winifred Fontana, 28 November 1934.
33. Ibid, to Hon. Francis Rodd, 23 November 1934.
34. Garnett, David (editor), op. cit., to K. W. Marshall, 18 May 1934.
35. Forster, E. M. 'Clouds Hill', *The Listener*, 1 September 1938, p.426.
36. Garnett, David (editor), op. cit., to Miss L. P. Black, 5 March 1934.
37. *T. E. Lawrence Papers*, op. cit., to Ernest Altounyan, 5 January 1933.
38. Garnett, David (editor), op. cit., to Edward Garnett, 10 August 1933.

Chapter 15 Retirement

1. Knowles, Patrick and Joyce, and Bob Hunt, *A Handful with Quietness*, p.23.
2. Brown, Malcolm (editor), *The Letters of T. E. Lawrence*, to Ezra Pound, 7 December 1934.
3. Ibid, to H. S. Ede, 3 January 1935.
4. Ibid, to Arthur Russell, 3 January 1935.
5. Ibid, to Eric Kennington, 6 August 1934.
6. Ibid, to Arthur Russell, 18 January 1935.
7. Garnett, David (editor), *The Letters of T. E. Lawrence*, draft of a letter to the Hon. Esmond Harmsworth, March 1935.
8. Knowles, Patrick and Joyce, and Bob Hunt, op. cit., p.36.
9 Garnett, David (editor), op. cit., to Pat Knowles, 19 March 1935.
10. Brown, Malcolm (editor), op. cit., to Winston Churchill, 19 March 1935.

11. Ibid, to Sir Evelyn Wrench, 1 April 1935.
12. Ibid, to George Brough, 5 April 1935.
13. Garnett, David (editor), op. cit., to Flight Lieutenant H. Norrington, 20 April 1935.
14. Ibid, to Lady Astor, 5 May 1935.
15. Ibid, to Eric Kennington, 6 May 1935.
16. Brown, Malcolm (editor), op. cit., to Eric Kennington, 6 May 1935.
17. Garnett, David (editor), op. cit., to E. M. Forster, 7 May 1935.
18. Brown, Malcolm (editor), op. cit., to E. 'Posh' Palmer, 10 May 1935.
19. Garnett, David (editor), op. cit., to Lady Astor, 8 May 1935, and p.537, Note 1.

Chapter 16 Lawrence's Love of Motorcycles

1. Lawrence, A. W. (editor), *T. E. Lawrence by His Friends,* p.111.
2. Ibid, p.143.
3. Brown, Malcolm (editor), *The Letters of T. E. Lawrence,* p.252.
4. Lawrence, A. W. (editor), op. cit., p.361.
5. Lawrence, A. W. (editor), op. cit., p.286.
6. Lawrence, T. E., *The Mint,* p.199.
7. Garnett, David (editor), *The Letters of T. E. Lawrence,* to George Brough, 27 September 1926.
8. Brown, Malcolm (editor), op. cit., p.399, note 3.
9. Ibid, to Sir Hugh Trenchard, 5 February 1929.
10. Winstein, Stephen, *Shaw's Corner,* p.82.
11. Brown, Malcolm (editor), op. cit., to Sir Hugh Trenchard, 16 April 1929.
12. From Brough Works Record Sheet, information kindly supplied by Jonathan M. Weekly
13. Garnett, David (editor), op. cit., to George Brough, 5 March 1932.
14. Brown, Malcolm (editor), op. cit., to George Brough, 3 May 1934.
15. Ibid, to Charlotte Shaw, 31 December 1934.
16. Mack, John E., *A Prince of Our Disorder: The Life of T. E. Lawrence,* p.451.
17. Garnett, David (editor), op. cit., p.487
18. Knowles, Patrick and Joyce, and Bob Hunt, *A Handful with Quietness,* p.37.
19. Brown, Malcolm (editor), op. cit., p.252.

Chapter 17 The Crash

1. Lawrence, A. W. (editor), *T. E. Lawrence by His Friends,* p.381
2. *Inquest Number 160, County of Dorset,* 21 May 1935.
3. Ibid.
4. Garnett, David (editor), *The Letters of T. E. Lawrence,* p.844.
5. Knowles, Patrick and Joyce, and Bob Hunt, *A Handful with Quietness,* p.42.
6. Ibid, p.44.
7. Corporal No. 7581979 Ernest Catchpole. Catchpole rose to the rank of staff

sergeant. He committed suicide at Cairo in July 1940 and was buried in Cairo's War Memorial Cemetery.

8. *Inquest Number 160*, op. cit.
9. *Daily Echo*, 15 May 1935.
10. *Inquest Number 160*, op. cit.
11. Albert Hargraves, interviewed by Stewart Rigby, 1982, in Marriott, Paul J., and Yvonne Argent, p.140.
12. Marriott, Paul J., and Yvonne Argent, *The Last Days of T. E. Lawrence: A Leaf in the Wind*, p.141.
13. Fletcher, Frank, statement to Bournemouth's *Daily Echo*, early 1985.
14. Fletcher, Frank, statement to Bournemouth's *Daily Echo*, 18 May 1985.
15. Joan Hughes, interviewed by Roland A. Hammersley, 10 February 1986, courtesy Wareham Town Museum.
16. Marriott, Paul J., and Yvonne Argent, op. cit., interview with Frank Fletcher, 13 August 1991, pp.130-7.
17. Knowles, Patrick and Joyce, and Bob Hunt, op. cit., p.46.
18. Marriott, Paul J., and Yvonne Argent, op. cit., interview with Frank Fletcher, 13 August 1991, p.144.
19. Ibid, interview with Frank Fletcher, 13 August 1991, pp.133-4.
20. Ibid, p.142.
21. Montague, Margaret, 'There was a Car', Bournemouth's *Daily Echo*, 5 September 1985.
22. Legg, Rodney, *Lawrence in Dorset*, p.113
23. Simpson, Andrew R. B., 'The Crash that Killed T. E. Lawrence', interview with Margaret Montague, November 1985, privately printed, in Marriott, Paul J., and Yvonne Argent, op. cit., p.146.

Chapter 18 A Reappraisal of the Crash

1. Marriott, Paul J., and Yvonne Argent, *The Last Days of T. E. Lawrence: A Leaf in the Wind*, p.149. Arthur Russell, interviewed by Malcolm Brown and Julia Cave, 30 May 1986.
2. Ibid, Map 8.
3. Roland A. Hammersley, sketch of crash site, based on his interview with Joan Hughes on 10 February 1986, courtesy Wareham Town Museum.
4. Information kindly supplied by Met. Office National Meteorological Archive. Times given are clock times – i.e. one hour ahead of GMT.
5. Information kindly supplied by Jonathan M. Weakly.
6. Marriott, Paul J., and Yvonne Argent, op. cit., Plates 39A, B and C.
7. Not including the fuel, the Brough weighed 440 lb. In contrast the weight of an errand boy's bicycle of the time was in the region of 60lb, with an additional 12 lb for the basket and, in Hargraves' case, an extra 15 lb for the 'parcel orders' – parcels of meat for delivery – (Marriott, Paul J., and Yvonne Argent, op. cit., p.131) making a total of 87 lb. (Based on the weight of a similar 1930s trades-

man's delivery bicycle, courtesy of Borough of Poole Museum Services.) This was probably not far short of the weight of Hargraves himself!

8. *Daily Telegraph*, report on the Inquest, 22 May 1935.

Chapter 19 The Exact Location of the Crash

1. This Ordnance Survey map was originally produced in 1901, but modified in 1927.
2. Lawrence's sketch of Clouds Hill, 17 April 1934, Marriott, Paul J., and Yvonne Argent, *The Last Days of T. E. Lawrence: A Leaf in the Wind*, Map 10.
3. RAF aerial photograph, 1947.
4. Google map, 2008.
5. Ibid.
6. Simpson, Andrew R. B., *Another Life: Lawrence After Arabia*, p. 233.
7. Marriott, Paul J., and Yvonne Argent, op. cit., Plate 35.
8. Ibid, Plate 38A.
9. Ibid, Plate 37A.
10. Ibid, Plate 36B.
11. Ibid, Plate 36A.
12. Based on the personal observations of the author.

Chapter 20 The Funeral: Aftermath

1. Bruce, John, 'Papers Relating to the Medical History of T. E. Lawrence', courtesy of the Imperial War Museum.
2. Legg, Rodney, *Lawrence in Dorset*, p.129.

3. Brady, Thomas J., 'Lawrence of Arabia and the Lure of the Roses', 18 August 1994, Philly.com

Chapter 21 The Effigy

1. Eric Kennington, 3 July 1945, Wareham. Courtesy of the Rector and Churchwardens of St Martin's-on-the-Walls, Wareham.
2. Knowles, Patrick and Joyce, and Bob Hunt, *A Handful with Quietness*, p.41.
3. *Story of the Lawrence Effigy*, told by Eric Kennington at Wareham on 3 July 1945. Courtesy of the Rector and Churchwardens of St Martin's-on-the-Walls, Wareham.
4. *Tale of an 'Arabian Knight': the T. E. Lawrence Effigy*, by Richard Knowles. *The T. E. Lawrence Society Journal*, 2:1.

Epilogue

1. Knowles, Patrick and Joyce, and Bob Hunt: E. V. G. Hunt: 'Pat Knowles of Clouds Hill', p.54.

BIBLIOGRAPHY

American Psychiatric Association, *Diagnostic and Statistical Manual of Mental Disorders* (DSM-IV-TR) (American Psychiatric Association, Washington, DC, 2000)

Atkins, Norman J., *Thomas Hardy and the Hardy Players* (Toucan Press, Guernsey, Channel Islands, UK, 1980)

Bell, Lady, (editor), *The Letters of Gertrude Bell* (Penguin, London, 1939)

Boyle, Andrew, *Trenchard: Man of Vision* (Collins, London, 1962)

Brame, Gloria D., William D. Brame, and Jon Jacobs, *Different Loving: The World of Sexual Dominance and Submission* (Villard, New York, 1993)

Brown, Malcolm, *The Letters of T. E. Lawrence* (J. M. Dent, London, 1988)

Brown, Malcolm and Julia Cave, *A Touch of Genius: The Life of T. E. Lawrence* (J.M. Dent, London, 1988)

Carter, Jan, *The Maltreated Child* (Priory Press, London, 1974)

Churchill, Winston, *Lawrence of Arabia as I Knew Him* (*Sunday Dispatch*, 19 May 1940)

Daily Echo, Bournemouth

Dixon, J & B. Jones (editors), *Macmillan Dictionary of National Biography, The* (Macmillan Reference Books, London, 1981)

Dunbar, Janet, *Mrs G.B.S.: A Biographical Portrait* (George G. Harrap, London, 1963)

Forty, George and Anne, *Bovington Tanks* (Wincanton Press, Wincanton, Somerset, 1988)

Forster, E. M., *Selected Letters of E. M. Forster* (Collins, London, 1985)

Gagnon, John H. and William Simon, *Sexual Conduct: The Social Sources of Human Sexuality* (Aldine Books, Chicago, 1973)

Garnett, David (editor), *The Letters of T. E. Lawrence* (Jonathan Cape, London, 1938)

Graves, Robert, *Lawrence and the Arabs* (Jonathan Cape, London, 1927)

Spencer, Gilbert RA, *Memoirs of a Painter* (Chatto & Windus, London, 1974)

Hart-Davis, Rupert (editor), *Siegfried Sassoon Diaries* (Faber & Faber, London, 1981, 1985)

Hirschfeld, Magnus, *Sexual Anomalies: The Origins, Nature, and Treatment of Sexual Disorders* (Emerson, New York, 1956)

Hogarth, D. G., *Mecca's Revolt Against the Turk* (*Century Magazine*, 100, London, 1920)

Human Rights Watch, *'No Escape: Male Rape in U.S. Prisons'* (Human Rights Watch, New York, April 2001)

James, Lawrence, *The Golden Warrior* (Weidenfield & Nicholson, London, 1990)

Knight, Ronald D., *T. E. Lawrence and the Max Gate Circle* (R. D. Knight, Bat & Ball Press, Weymouth, Dorset, 1995)

Knightley, Philip & Colin Simpson (*Sunday Times Weekly Review*, 23 and 30 June, and 7 and 14 September 1968)

Knowles, Patrick and Joyce, and Bob Hunt, *A Handful with Quietness* (E. V. G. Hunt, Weymouth, March 1992)

Korda, Michael, *Hero: The Life and Legend of Lawrence of Arabia* (JR Books, London, 2010)

Koss, Mary P. and Mary R. Harvey, *The Rape Victim, Clinical and Community Interventions*, New York: Sage Library of Social Research 185 (Sage, London, 1991)

Krafft-Ebing, Richard von, *Psychopathia Sensualis: eine Klinisch-Forensische Studie* (Arcade Publishing, New York, 1998)

Lawrence, A. W. (editor), *Letters to T. E. Lawrence* (Jonathan Cape, London, 1962)

Lawrence, A. W. (editor), *Oriental Assembly by T. E. Lawrence* (Williams and Norgate, London, 1939)

Lawrence, A. W. (editor), *Secret Dispatches from Arabia* (Golden Cockerell, London, 1939)

Lawrence, A. W. (editor), *T. E. Lawrence by His Friends* (McGraw-Hill, New York, 1963)

Lawrence, M. R. (editor), *The Home Letters of T. E. Lawrence and his Brothers* (Macmillan, Oxford, 1954)

Lawrence, T. E., *'An Essay on Flecker'* (Corvinus Press, London, 1937)

Lawrence, T. E., *Seven Pillars of Wisdom* (Jonathan Cape, London, 1935)

Lawrence, T. E., *Minorities*, edited by J. M. Wilson, (Jonathan Cape, London, 1971)

Lawrence, T. E., *The Mint* (Jonathan Cape, London, 1955)

Legg, Rodney, *Lawrence in Dorset* (Dorset Publishing Company, Wincanton, Somerset, 1997)

Liddel Hart, Basil, *T. E. Lawrence to his Biographer* (Liddel Hart, London, 1938)

Mack, John E., *A Prince of Our Disorder: The Life of T. E. Lawrence* (Weidenfeld & Nicholson, London, 1976)

Marriott, Paul J., and Yvonne Argent, *The Last Days of T. E. Lawrence: A Leaf in the Wind*, (Alpha Press, Portland, Oregon, 1996)

McMullen, Richie J., *Male Rape* (GMP Publishers, London, 1990)

Orlans, Harold, *Biography of a Broken Hero* (McFarland, Jefferson, North Carolina, U.S.A., 2002)

Rousseau, Jean-Jacques, *The Confessions of Jean-Jacques Rousseau* (Privately printed for members of the Aldus Society, London, 1903)

Scarce, Michael, *Male on Male Rape* (Plenum Press, New York, 1997)

Stewart, Desmond, *T. E. Lawrence* (Paladin, London, 1979)

Sunday Express

Inquest Number 160, County of Dorset, 21 May 1935

Sassoon, Siegfried, *Diaries* (Faber & Faber, London, 1924)

Scarce, Michael, *Male on Male Rape* (Perseus Books Group, New York, 1997)

Schwartz, Dr Allan N., LCSW, Ph.D., 'A Discussion of Sexual Fetishism and Masochism', updated 20 May 2008 (Online)

Simpson, Andrew R. B., *Another Life: Lawrence After Arabia* (Spellmount, Stroud, 2011)

Smith, Clare Sydney, *The Golden Reign* (Cassell, London 1978)

Soanes, Catherine and Angus Stevenson, *Oxford Dictionary of English* (Oxford University Press, 2006)

Titterington, Ellen E., 'The Domestic Life of Thomas Hardy'. *Thomas Hardy Year Book*, Monograph 4, courtesy of G. Stevens Cox MA (Oxon) Ph.D., editor (Toucan Press, Guernsey, Channel Islands, UK, 1963)

Townsend, Larry, *The Leatherman's Handbook* (Modernismo Publications, New York, 1983)

Wilson, Jeremy, *Lawrence of Arabia* (Heinemann, London, 1989)

Wilson, Jeremy and Nicole (editors), *T. E. Lawrence: Correspondence with Bernard and Charlotte Shaw 1922-1926* (Castle Hill, Woodgreen Common, Hants, 2000)

Winstein, Stephen, *Shaw's Corner* (Hutchinson, London, 1952)

INDEX